The Caribbean Cruising Handbook

Also by Bill Robinson

Islands

Where to Cruise

South to the Caribbean

Cruising: The Boats and the Places

Where the Trade Winds Blow:
A Yachting Guide to Southern Waters

The Caribbean Cruising Handbook

A Planning Guide for Charterers and Private Owners

Bill Robinson

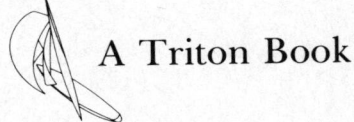

A Triton Book

Dodd, Mead & Company
NEW YORK

Copyright © 1986 by Bill Robinson

All rights reserved

No part of this book may be reproduced in any form without permission in writing from the publisher.
Published by Dodd, Mead & Company, Inc.
79 Madison Avenue, New York, N.Y. 10016
Distributed in Canada by
McClelland and Stewart Limited, Toronto
Manufactured in the United States of America
Designed by Erich Hobbing

First Edition

Library of Congress Cataloging-in-Publication Data

Robinson, Bill, 1918–
   The Caribbean cruising handbook.

  Bibliography: p.
1. Yachts and yachting—Caribbean Area.
2. Sailboats—Chartering—Caribbean Area.
3. Caribbean Area—Description and travel—
1981–   . I. Title.
GV817.C37R59 1986   797.1'09729   85-24724
ISBN 0–396–08735–3 (pbk.)

1 2 3 4 5 6 7 8 9 10

Contents

Preface vii
I The Caribbean 1
II Getting There—and What to Bring 14
III Chartering 26
IV Operating a Private Boat 41
V The Islands Profiled 46
VI Support Systems 77
VII Eating Ashore 85
VIII Anchoring 94
IX Practical Matters 101
X Suggested Itineraries 118
Bibliography 127
List of Cruising Guides 129

Preface

This is a "before you go" as well as a "while you are there" book. It is intended as an advance-planning guide to help you decide the where, when, how, and what of a Caribbean cruise. (The why is easy: the Caribbean is a great cruising area, and a wonderful change, in winter, from northern climates.) It should help you choose the type of charter boat and the charter area that are best for you. If you are taking your own boat, there is advice on what is involved in operating it down there. Once you are there, this book will help to fill you in on the islands and tell you what to look for, but actual navigation should be done with the aid of the cruising guides listed in the Bibliography.

The book is based on personal experience going back to wartime duty in 1942 and various charter cruises starting in 1961. We have based our own boat, the CSY 37 cutter *Brunelle*, there since 1979.

I hope you will enjoy the Caribbean as much as I have.

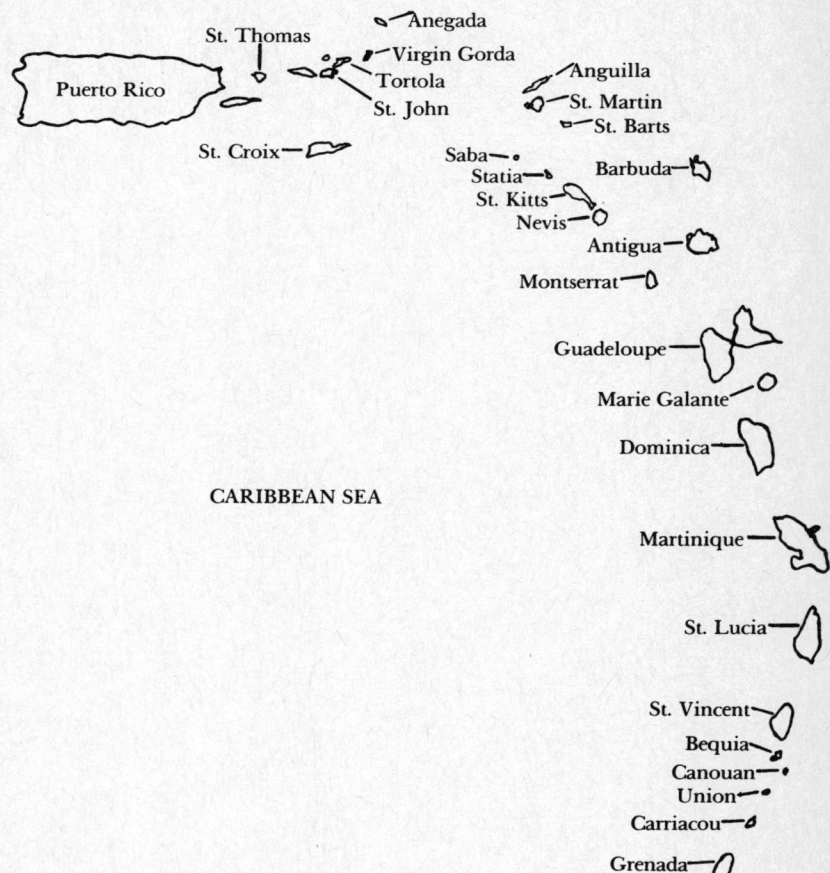

The Caribbean Cruising Handbook

I

The Caribbean

The Caribbean Sea combines all the elements that make for great cruising, and it is readily at hand in this jet age from all parts of North and South America and from Europe. The climate, the trade winds, the abundance and variety of harbors, the amount of sunshine, the relative ease of navigation, and the availability of hundreds of charter yachts, both bareboat and crewed, cannot be matched in any other area. And although the sea routes to it can be a real challenge, the Caribbean Sea is also close enough for many private owners to make their way there in their own boats.

This island-ringed sea is almost two thousand miles on an east-west axis, and over seven hundred miles at its widest point. Lying between 9° and 21° north latitude and 60° and 84° west longitude, it is completely in the Tropics. The islands that enclose it present vivid contrasts in physical makeup, culture, lifestyle, and political orientation, but they all share legendary charms of sun, sand, and sea. To the sailor seeking change, challenge, adventure, and relaxation—the perfect escape—they are unmatched.

One of the first problems encountered is how to pronounce "Caribbean." The even split on the matter leaves this up to personal choice. My favorite example of this is in the daily 0800 weather forecast from the commercial radio station in St. Thomas, American Virgins. The announcer says, "We now bring you the latest weather forecast for the eastern Caribbean," and the man reading the weather report then says, "Here is the weather for the Eastern Caribbean." I personally prefer the latter, but there doesn't seem to be any hard and fast rule.

There are many contrasts: the ten-thousand-foot mountains of Hispaniola and the low sands of Anegada and Barbuda, barely above the water; the urban bustle of San Juan and the lonely isolation of the reef off Belize; the sophistication of Martinique and the simple ways of Dominica, just forty miles to the north; the Spanish rhythms of the Dominican Republic, Puerto Rico, and Central America, and the calypso of Trinidad; the communism of Cuba and Nicaragua and the British colonialism of Anguilla and Montserrat, or the democracies of many other islands. In a day's passage between islands, as in the one between Dominica and Martinique, there can be a complete change in culture and atmosphere—one of the fascinations of ranging the Caribbean on a cruise.

The Geography

Just ninety miles from Florida, the first chain of islands enclosing the Caribbean, the Greater Antilles, starts with Cuba and continues eastward through the big, mountainous islands of Hispaniola, shared politically by Haiti and the Dominican Republic, to Puerto Rico. Jamaica, off by itself to the south of Cuba, is also considered a part of the Greater Antilles.

The Virgin Islands, American and British, lie just east of Puerto Rico. There is then an eighty-mile open-water gap, Anegada Passage, to St. Martin, where the four-hundred-mile chain of the Lesser Antilles starts. These mostly volcanic, mountainous islands run southeastward to Antigua, then north and south to Grenada, ninety miles from the South American continent and Venezuela. Trinidad-Tobago is part of the Caribbean world, although not in a technical, geographic sense. These islands are nestled just off the Venezuelan coast, ninety miles southeast of Grenada. Barbados, the same distance off to the east in the Atlantic, is also considered a part of the Caribbean, though also not geographically.

When the British ruled most of the Caribbean area, they split the Lesser Antilles into two groups—the Leeward and Windward Islands; it is more of a political convenience than an accurate geographical description. The Leewards are the northern islands between Anguilla and Guadeloupe Channel, the Windwards the southern islands. This designation might be accurate geographically during the summer months, when the trades tend to be south of east, but the reverse can be true in the winter, when there is more north to the trades.

From Grenada westward along the Venezuelan coast, the "ABC" Dutch islands—Aruba, Bonaire, and Curaçao—string along the classical Spanish Main, while inshore there are many islands off Venezuela, with Margarita the largest. Venezuela and Colombia are the only South American countries bordering the Caribbean, and they offer a distinct contrast to the island life offshore. Although boating facilities are relatively undeveloped, Venezuela has good cruising waters among its islands. Colombia, on the other hand, has for years been off-limits to yachts carrying insurance because of the drug trade, and is devoid of coastal islands. Also, for sailors, the Spanish Main is strictly a one-way street, downwind to westward. This is an area of very strong trade winds, and trying to go eastward into them is virtually impossible in a yacht.

The western Caribbean does not have much to offer the cruising yachtsman, either physically or politically, until the San Blas Islands off the coast of Panama. One is almost completely on one's own in the San Blas, which do have great scenery, good protection behind the fringing reef that extends for most of their one-hundred-mile string, and a glimpse at the pre-Colombian life of the Cuna Indians. (This has been changed in certain areas by visits from cruise ships and by disruptive influences from the mainland, but it is still one of the longest-lasting primitive societies in this hemisphere.)

Not until the Bay Islands of Honduras, well up the Central American isthmus, and the reef off Belize are there waters well adapted to vacation cruising between closely spaced ports and anchorages. The Yucatán Peninsula, jutting out from Mexico north of the Gulf of Honduras, marks the western end of the Caribbean; here the developed resorts, such as Cancún, Cozumel, and Isla Mujeres, are mainly oriented toward sportfishing as an attraction for visitors.

That, briefly, is the lay of the land in the Caribbean basin. Individual islands and cruising areas will be described in more detail in later chapters.

The History

As one sails through the islands of the Caribbean, one cannot help but be aware of their colorful, often bloody history, which has been in a state of flux, ever rife with new developments, from the first voyages of Columbus.

Named for the Carib Indians, who, along with the Arawaks, were native to the area, the Caribbean was thrust violently into the early history of this hemisphere by the accidental landfall of Columbus in its latitudes. (The alternate name of West Indies comes, of course, from the original supposition that Columbus had found the East Indies.)

The Spaniards had first licks in the wake of Columbus, and in their greed for gold and other spoils, they virtually wiped out the Caribs and Arawaks by forcing them into slave labor, as well as ending, as such, the Indian civilizations of the mainland. The British, French, and Dutch were not long in competing with the Spaniards and each other for control of a region that had the same economic impact in its day as the oil-producing areas of the world have in modern times.

Islands changed hands frequently in a bloody game of musical chairs. From the days of Sir Francis Drake and Henry Morgan through the period of the American Revolution, the exploits of Rodney and Nelson, and the Napoleonic Wars, the rivalries and conflicts of Europe spilled over to the sunny waters and shores of the Caribbean. St. Lucia (pronounced *"loo-*sha"), for instance, changed hands more than a dozen times, a conflict that still shows in local place names and language.

By the mid-nineteenth century, the colonial alignment had stabilized somewhat, to remain largely at status quo through World War II. The Spanish presence finally ended with the Spanish-American War closing out the nineteenth century, putting the United States into the picture. In 1917, the United States purchased the American Virgins from Denmark. There were other minor changes, such as Sweden's sale of St. Barthélemy to France in the 1870s, and by the end of World War I, England, France, Holland, and the United States were the remaining powers in the area.

Since World War II, the former British colonies have gradually gained independence from the Commonwealth, leaving just Anguilla, Montserrat, and the British Virgins as colonies. This proliferation of independent nations has had the effect on the cruising yachtsman of adding to the responsibilities for entering and clearing all the political entities—and expanding his locker of courtesy flags.

Of profound influence on the Caribbean was the importation of slaves from Africa to work the sugar, cotton, and tobacco plantations that were so economically important in the seventeenth and eighteenth centuries and on into the nineteenth. With the native populations wiped out by the Spaniards, slaves became the cheap labor necessary to carry on the economy. Now, the "natives" are mostly descendants of the African slaves.

Slavery, accepted though it was at the time, was a brutal way of life, and led to violent revolts and uprisings, such as the one in Haiti that killed every white on the island and has kept it a black, independent country for almost two hundred years. England freed her slaves in the 1830s, but the political independence that gradually followed throughout the islands has aggravated, rather than solved, economic woes, and unemployment is a serious problem in the area today. The cruising sailor sees evidence of this in the "rowboat mafia" of youngsters who harass yachts entering harbors in the lower Caribbean, trying to make a buck in any way possible by offering all sorts of services and local items for sale.

Given this condition on islands that are 90 percent or more black (with St. Barthélemy—or St. Barts—the exception in reverse proportion), one might expect racial tensions to be a problem. Indeed, the prevailing racial climate on a given island can change radically in a short time, and there have been instances of islands going through a "black power" period that made things unpleasant for visitors. But this unrest is usually short-lived. The average West Indian is an outgoing, polite person, eager to be friends if treated with friendship and respect. The vast majority want visitors to feel welcome on their island, as long as it is recognized that it *is* their island. The simple amenities of a polite greeting and a smile, an exchange of pleasantries, and thank you's when appropriate go a long way toward smoothing relations. As in every area of the modern world, there is some crime, but no more than in many American neighborhoods, and, in fact, a lot less than some. Simple precautions should always be taken about safeguarding valuables.

That the status quo is never guaranteed cannot be better illustrated than by the recent history of Grenada ("gren-*aid*-uh"), climaxing in the Intervention (as Grenadians prefer to call it) in October 1983. The Caribbean will continue to be an area of unrest and ferment, though certainly much less violent in those respects than many other parts of the globe, and not enough to negate its powerful attraction for the sailor.

The Climate

Generally speaking, the climate of the Caribbean basin is all of a piece, the powerful easterly trade wind the dominant natural force. Because of the trade wind, Caribbean weather is predictable and reliable. About 90 percent of the time the wind blows from somewhere between northeast and southeast (and most usually due east) at about 14 to 18 knots, with sunny skies, puffy clouds that contain isolated, one-cloud showers, and whitecapped seas. In the breeze, the temperature will be 80 to 86 degrees Fahrenheit during the day, and 6 to 8 degrees lower at night all year round. At sea, anything below 70 or above 80 degrees is a distinct rarity, and it is usually cooler at sea in the Caribbean in midsummer than in many North American land areas.

There are some seasonal and geographic variations. The fall is the rainy season, and late summer into fall is the hurricane season. Hurricanes are a menace in the Caribbean and are watched with great care and respect, but they do not hit any one island or region with any more regularity than one would hit, say, Providence, Rhode Island. That the unusual *can* happen was graphically illustrated in 1984 by Hurricane Klaus, which was spawned south of Puerto Rico out of a rainy low-pressure system in November, when hurricanes are supposedly finished, and proceeded to sweep *eastward* out of the area, against all known records of hurricane behavior. It eventually went all the way across to Spain and into the Mediterranean, raising havoc on the Aegean coast of Turkey a week later.

Nature does have its freaks. In my experience of the Caribbean going back to 1942, I've seen the wind blow from every point of the compass at one time or another. So, too, there have been days of flat calm (but not many). I have fortunately not experienced a hurricane in the Caribbean, but I've seen winds over fifty knots, two days of rain that produced seventeen inches, and, three times in six years, visibility reduced down to three or four miles because of sandstorms from Africa suspended in the air and carried all the way across the Atlantic by the trades.

Winter northers from the continent can reach down as far as the northern tier of Caribbean islands, bringing a spell of strong north winds and big swells two or three times a winter. Northers also can sweep down on the western Caribbean's Gulf of Honduras with cold winds and rain. Sometimes, in the winter months, the wind may be a normal trade from the east, but northerly swells from an Atlantic disturbance may roll in on the north side of the upper tier islands and sometimes as far down as Antigua. Fog is unheard of, but heavy rain can hamper visibility.

When the trades are blowing from the east, especially in winter, an "easterly wave" might develop, more or less like a curl on a cold front, and bring a day or two of steady rain and higher winds. There have been weeks when visitors experienced rain for the entire time, or excessively high winds for several days, making sailing less pleasant than normal. Traditionally, there is a period of strong winds over the change of the year, known as the "Christmas winds." Some years they are on schedule, while in others they never appear, or don't appear until February. When they do appear, the velocity of the trades increases from under twenty knots to the mid to high twenties.

All these exceptions fall into that abnormal 10 percent of Caribbean weather. It is bad luck to encounter one of these weather situations, but anyone who has sailed for any length of time knows that there must always be an expectation of the unexpected.

A major factor in the climate, in addition to the trade wind, is the bright, tropical sun. One of the easiest ways to ruin a vacation cruise is to overdo sun exposure on the first day or two. Pale northerners reveling in the sudden change from winter at home sometimes can't resist basking in the sun, and they often pay for it. Judicious use of sun creams and protective clothing, especially a hat in the direct sun, is vitally important. Even under a Bimini top, which most charter boats have, the reflected rays off the water can burn severely. A gradual tanning process, erring on the safe side, is the best way to get a tan without burning. (British Virgin Islanders, incidentally, call a tree whose bark is always peeling, revealing shiny red wood underneath, a "tourist tree.") Eye protection is also important. Again, the reflected rays off the water can be just as bothersome as the direct sun.

There is one phenomenon of tropical weather that often disconcerts visitors. Just after sunset, when the heat of the sun suddenly goes out of the air, the temperature will drop several degrees quickly while the breeze continues to blow, and the result is a temporary wind-chill factor out of proportion to the temperature change. The effect can be quite a shock, like walking from a hot sidewalk into an air-conditioned room, and often misleads people into taking extra clothing if they are going ashore or to another boat. In fact, the new temperature is still the pleasant warmth of a tropical night, and the body soon adjusts.

Another weather phenomenon of the Caribbean area is the green flash. Some people who have never seen it insist that it's a myth, but it *can* be seen on occasion, and is a scientific fact. It comes at sunset (or sunrise) as the top rim of the sun is at the horizon. The horizon must be free of clouds, and the atmosphere must be clear and reddish. If these conditions exist, and you don't blink at the wrong moment, the top edge of the sun will turn a brilliant, liquid green just as it disappears at sunset or first appears at sunrise. On rare occasions, there is even a ray of green light in the sky above the sun. The explanation for the green flash is that the colors of the spectrum are refracted differently in the dense surface atmosphere, and green is the only one that penetrates right at the surface.

If you're standing at sea level near a building with outside stairs, it's a good trick to see the flash down below, then dash up the stairs and see it again. The reason it is seen less often at sunrise in the Caribbean is that, aside from people still being asleep, most of the harbors have land to the eastward, and one must be at sea at dawn to have the proper horizon.

Sailing Conditions

From the foregoing descriptions of geography and climate, it's not too hard to imagine the sailing conditions in the Caribbean. Obviously, there's plenty of wind. Calm days are rare, and the general expectation is for fourteen knots and up, with the need to be ready for heavier winds some of the time. During normal weather, the wind will be steadily from the east. There will be puffy, trade-wind cumulus clouds, good visibility, and occasional one-cloud rain squalls. The wind will pick up for a short period as the squall approaches, there will be a brief but sharp pelting from surprisingly cold rain, and the squall will sweep on by quickly, with bright sun taking over again. Very rarely will a squall be thick enough and last long enough to reduce visibility seriously, but I've seen zero visibility in heavy rain last as long as half an hour, so it's always good to have an idea of where you are if there are any hazards near.

There are lifts and puffs in the trade wind, varying a few degrees, and it is always worthwhile to watch for them and play them. Sudden wind shifts are truly rare except in the vicinity of a developing squall. Thunderstorms are relatively rare, especially in the winter. Near high islands, the wind can do all sorts of strange things on the leeward side, where there can be anything from a flat calm to rather strong reverse winds in from the west. It's not uncommon for harbors in the lee of high hills to the east to have a constant backwind from the west, and this can affect both sailing and anchoring.

In some places the leeward side of these hills can be an area of sudden, vicious "williwaws," strong blasts of air rushing down from the peaks with unsuspected violence. The south end of Dominica, the Pitons of St. Lucia, and Charleston Harbor on Canouan in the Grenadines are three places I've experienced this phenomenon. Of course, the strength of the trade wind blowing unimpeded against the windward side of these areas has a great deal to do with the strength of the williwaws.

With all this wind as a general condition in the Caribbean, there is bound to be some rough sea. It all depends on where you are in relation to the land. The leeward sides of the islands seldom have whitecapped chop. The waves are skittish and irregular as vagrant puffs find their way to the water. Sometimes there is a heavy surge that works its way around to the leeward sides of the islands and makes itself felt in harbors. At one time or another, surge can be a problem in all but a handful of Caribbean harbors. Very few harbors are protected from all directions, and the ones that are so protected are extremely popular and crowded.

In parts of the British Virgins and the Grenadines, to name two of the most popular cruising areas, there is enough protection from surrounding islands to create an "inland sea," with delightful conditions—a good breeze and smooth water. Even in these relatively protected areas, however, there is suddenly an exposure to the open sea between islands, and smooth water quickly turns choppy.

In the open-sea passages between the islands, it's almost always rough. The waves have had a good run all the way from Africa, and they have an authority that

The Caribbean

makes itself felt. They aren't dangerous, but they're big, blue, and wet, topped by foaming whitecaps. You know you're at sea, in true Caribbean conditions, when you're in one of these inter-island channels.

II

Getting There— and What to Bring

As mentioned in the previous chapter, the Caribbean is today easily accessible from all directions. And since most of the sailing done there is in charter yachts by people who fly in for a cruise of a week or two, accessibility is an important factor in the Caribbean's popularity with sailors.

By Air

San Juan is the hub of Caribbean air travel, flights arriving from most mainland areas either direct or through New York, Miami, or Atlanta. The New York–San Juan flight is 1,399 statute miles, Miami–San Juan roughly a thousand miles. From San Juan there are connections to smaller outlying islands. There are also flights direct to San Juan from several different European cities. Planes from Europe also come to St. Martin, Antigua, Guadeloupe, Martinique, and Barbados. Those islands, and others like St. Thomas, St. Croix, St. Lucia, Jamaica, and the Dutch ABC islands, have nonstop or through-plane service from the U.S. mainland. Almost all the islands, even tiny ones like Anegada, Saba, Barbuda, and Carriacou, have connecting services on local airlines. The island with no airstrip at all, like Bequia, is rare.

Getting There—and What to Bring

Arranging the best flight for convenience and cost can be a tricky problem, as there is an amazing discrepancy in fares charged on different routes and at different times, as well as special excursion fares, advance-purchase fares, and tour packages. Most of the bareboat charter companies have their own or a cooperating travel agency that can arrange special excursion fares and save the charterer a great deal of money, and such plans are worth advance investigation. Charter companies also usually arrange ground transportation at both ends of a trip, especially important at the Caribbean end. Here buses or taxis operated by the charter company meet flights and take passengers directly to the boat, usually at no extra cost, a reassuring way to arrive in a strange area. If you are on your own in getting a taxi, it's wise to establish the fare ahead of time. Though most islands with a steady tourist trade have set fares for standard trips that are posted in airports or at tourist bureaus, there are taxi drivers who do not follow them. Passengers going to professionally operated charter boats or to private yachts will normally be on their own in getting ground transportation, and should take note of posted taxi fares. Taxi drivers usually expect a tip, but perhaps shouldn't be given one if the fare is excessive.

The major airlines running to the big airports operate in standard airline fashion, and a flight to the Caribbean is no different than a flight from, say, New York to Los Angeles. However, luggage handing at some of the airports, particularly San Juan, is not the most reliable, and it's usually risky business to check baggage through a connection, such as New York–San Juan–British Virgins. Despite the nuisance, it's better to check luggage flight by flight, personally supervising the transfer. Even with this method, it's important to bring essentials, such as medicines and overnight equipment like toothbrush, shaving gear, and so forth in hand luggage. It's also smart to have at least a T-shirt and/or blouse and bathing suit with you, so you don't have to sit around in city clothes waiting for luggage that has gone astray.

Along the same lines, the local airlines that island-hop around the Caribbean tend to be a bit haphazard in their operations. This doesn't refer to unsafe mechanical standards or operating procedures, but rather to schedule keeping, baggage handling, and the level of service at ticket counters. It's important to remember that the island pace is slow and relaxed, even when you're in a hurry, and can be frustrating, especially when things go awry and "nobody knows from nuttin'." The only solution is to try to relax and adopt the island pace yourself. Obviously, it's best to allow extra time when checking in with the local airlines, and to have tickets and documents ready and in order.

All this is not to discourage anyone from taking such a trip, merely a word of warning on how to operate and what to expect. One thing there is seldom any worry about is weather delays. On occasion, rain squalls will delay operations, but normally the delays are due to the pace set by humans.

For the rare person who will not fly, the Caribbean is not impossible to reach. One can take a train to Miami and work out an arrangement with a cruise line whose ships touch regularly at Caribbean ports.

By Sea

More and more people are bringing their own boats to the Caribbean. As I mentioned in Chapter I, this can be quite a challenge, but it is certainly worth considering for those with the time (and the experience) to ven-

Getting There—and What to Bring

ture offshore. Unfortunately, some unqualified people have jumped into such a project without studying what is required in the way of their boats' seaworthiness and their own knowledge, and each fall sees boats lost or in distress and in need of rescue while trying to get to the islands.

Interestingly, it's about as easy (although of course more time-consuming) to bring a boat from Europe as it is to come down from the States. The classic route is to head southward to the Canary Islands or Cape Verde Islands (which can be the roughest part of the voyage from European ports), then head westward in the trade winds to the Caribbean. If the trades are behaving normally, this is a pleasant downwind slide of somewhere close to three weeks, depending on the size of the boat and how much her crew gets out of her. A great many boats do come over from Europe this way—some that look as though they should have stayed in port.

From the States, there are any number of approaches to the Caribbean. The most ambitious, of course, is to bring a boat from the Pacific coast. This entails a long passage down the Central American coast, transit of the Panama Canal (which may become more difficult as the local government takes control), and then a slug up the Caribbean to the cruising areas. As mentioned earlier, it's virtually impossible to thrash your way to windward past Colombia and Venezuela for about a thousand miles to get to the islands. (One wonders how Columbus ever negotiated this route, which he did, painfully, over a long period of time in his clumsy caravels.) From the Canal, the only thing to do is head northeast across the open Caribbean, perhaps for the Virgins, hoping that the wind isn't too far in the north, which would make it a real beat. At best, it would be a wet, rough close reach, but plenty of boats have accomplished it. An alternative would be to head as far north as Jamaica, then work gradually east along the islands.

The bulk of traffic comes from the East Coast, anywhere from Maine to Florida. There are several ways of accomplishing this approach. Aside from the route chosen, the timing is also important. Many inexperienced people, usually in unsuitable boats, head offshore for the islands in the autumn from the Northeast, but a good bit of luck is needed to negotiate an offshore passage safely at that time. There's a very small time lag between the hurricane season, which extends into October, and the autumn storms that rage up the seaboard with the intensity of hurricanes, but without the fanfare.

A study of weather records shows that there is usually one major coastal storm sometime between the third week of October and mid-November, very often developing so rapidly in the unstable weather patterns near Cape Hatteras that it gives weather forecasters only a few hours of advance notice. Time and again, this storm has caught yachts on the offshore passage between the East Coast and Bermuda, and there has been at least a tragedy a year as a result. Venturing from the Northeast to Bermuda any time in the autumn is risky business. Hundreds of boats have made it, usually after a hair-raising experience on the way, but many have not. The crew must be fully experienced in offshore passaging, and the boat must be sound, well-found, and properly equipped to attempt it.

The next alternative, and the recommended route for an offshore passage to the islands, is to go inside, via the Intracoastal Waterway, to Morehead City, North Carolina, in mid-October, then play the weather forecasts for a departure from there. The trick is to pick an offshore breeze to depart in—a cold-front northwester

Getting There—and What to Bring

is best—and carry it as far as possible on a run, making easting. The normal pattern is for the northwester to move around into the southwest as the pressure system moves offshore, providing a good reaching breeze for more easting across the Gulf Stream. Then, when the longitude of the Virgin Islands is reached, the boat is turned south, in an easterly trade wind by now, it is hoped, for a reach down to the islands. This is a wonderful scenario, and it works a good percentage of the time, but there have been myriad variations and plenty of boats lost or severely buffeted in attempting to carry it out.

Offshore departure from farther down the seaboard just means a longer open-water passage and is not very practical. The coastline tends sharply to the southwest south of Morehead City, increasing the rhumb-line distance offshore rapidly. The next most practical area for departure is southern Florida.

A boat from the north can get to Florida by using the Intracoastal Waterway inside all the way—a long, sometimes tedious trip, but a safe and protected one, with some interesting sights and experiences along the way. In good weather, it's possible to make an occasional offshore run between inlets to alter the routine of chugging down the ICW. Then, from south Florida, there are more alternatives for heading to the islands. The basic choice is between an offshore passage and island-hopping. Because of the way the coastline has receded westward south of the Carolinas, the offshore run from Florida is almost as long as the one from Morehead, but chances are that the weather will be better on the run from Florida.

Again, the trick is to pick a good weather pattern for departure, waiting for a cold front to provide a northwester. This is then carried as far as possible through the Bahamas and on out into the Atlantic until the trade winds are met. If there is a northeasterly slant to them, it should be possible to head for the Virgins on a close reach on the port tack, but more often there is some windward work to be done, and it can be a tough slug if the trades have their full strength. There are also such navigational hazards as the Silver Bank, eighty miles north of the Dominican Republic. Still, the percentages are better than the Morehead route for avoiding storms, and the weather will be a lot warmer no matter what the point of sailing is.

Finally, there is the island-hopping route from Florida. Boating author Carleton Mitchell has dubbed this route "The Thorny Path," as it is usually all to windward. The advantages are that the runs can be short, with plenty of harbors on the way, as opposed to the nonstop route, and the harbors are often interesting in themselves, well worth a visit.

If you're in a hurry, the island-hopping route is not recommended, because the weather must be waited out quite often, and, as I've said, it's tempting to explore the various harbors along the way. We chose to island-hop when we took our own CSY 37, *Brunelle,* from Tampa to the Virgin Islands in January 1979. We had all winter to do it, and so spent lots of time in Bahamian harbors along the way, as well as in the Turks and Caicos and the Dominican Republic. As a result, it was not an arduous thrash.

After lingering in the Bahamas, enjoying the Exumas especially, we finally set out southeastward from George Town, Great Exuma, and from then on made as much progress as we could without pushing against questionable weather. It was a hard two-day slug from Long Island through the lower Bahamas to Providen-

Getting There—and What to Bring

ciales in the Caicos, with a northeaster that piped up over thirty knots on occasion, giving us a tough close reach. After waiting out the weather and a crew change in the Caicos for a week, we hit a twenty-four-hour calm and powered most of the way to Puerto Plata in the Dominican Republic over what could have been the toughest windward work of the trip, 150 miles, if the normal trades had been blowing.

Once in Puerto Plata we had broken the back of the trip, although Mona Passage between Hispaniola and San Juan, 180 miles to windward over a notoriously rugged stretch of water, was far from easy.

There are variations on this trip, such as ducking down farther westward in the Bahamas to Great Inagua and then Haiti, which involves shorter passages but a longer windward push along the forbidding north coast of Hispaniola, and uncertainties about what kind of reception might be encountered in Haiti. One can also go south through Mona Passage and along the south coast of Puerto Rico.

Each of these routes to the islands has its advantages and drawbacks. All have been successfully negotiated by hundreds of boats, yet all have produced disappointments, failures, and even tragedies. To make a choice, it's necessary to weigh many factors, such as time available, ability of crew and boat to handle offshore passages, the sailing capability of the boat, and how tough the crew feels. We enjoyed our version of The Thorny Path because it wasn't too thorny. In another year it might have produced a different and less pleasant set of experiences.

No matter how the Caribbean has been reached, there's hardly anyone who will say that the effort wasn't worth it.

What to Bring

The basic rules that apply to all things when packing for the Caribbean are "When in doubt, leave it out" and "Least is best."

Depending on how you look at it, with cynicism or sympathy, one of the more daunting sights in the Caribbean is of some groups of newcomers arriving for a charter, with mountains of hard suitcases trundling down the pier behind them. One can imagine the scene as the desperate skipper tries to figure out where to stow the bulky stuff and cringes for his cabin soles as the charterers step aboard in hard shoes and teetery high heels.

Experienced sailors are familiar with the problem of luggage aboard and excess gear, and usually arrive with efficient-looking duffels in a manageable amount, but even veteran sailors sometimes bring too much with them when they pack for a Caribbean sail. The basics are a T-shirt and a bathing suit; those who have spent a lot of time in the islands know that a minimum of these items will last a long time. Laundry service is not hard to come by, and on-board laundering is easy, as the sun and breeze are extremely efficient drying agents. There's almost no need for warm clothing. A light sweater or flyweight windbreaker will take care of any chill encountered. Some boats provide foul-weather gear, but it's seldom needed for any length of time, and the lightest kind of parka will take care of most situations.

People coming from a cold, midwinter climate often bring their heavy coats and city clothes with them when they come south. This should be avoided if possible. Usually, transportation to and from the northern airport can be arranged so that nobody is outdoors for any length of time.

Getting There—and What to Bring

Luggage should be soft and foldable for on-board stowage, and for convenience, if possible, should be limited to the carry-on variety. I know experienced sailors who have worked this down to a science, knowing exactly what their minimum needs are in sailing clothes, so that they don't have to be bothered with checked luggage. This may not be possible in all cases, but, again, at least medicines and overnight essentials should be kept in hand luggage.

The essentials of a Caribbean sailing wardrobe are a few light T-shirts or polo shirts, shorts, and a bathing suit. Men may want one pair of lightweight slacks for going ashore in the evenings, but they're not a necessity, and women can get by with a couple of light skirts and blouses. Almost nowhere are a coat and tie necessary, and places that require such dress can be conveniently boycotted by sailors, as the climate usually makes it a bit uncomfortable anyway. A Caribbean sailing cruise is probably not the right sort of vacation for someone who feels the need to dress for show.

Those who are especially susceptible to sunburn should have long-sleeved shirts and leg coverage, plus a good sun hat. It's a good idea to bring your own sun protection, and it's important to know your own susceptibility and tolerance. The kind of lotion that suits you best may not be available, even in the well-stocked drugstores in all sailing centers. It's also smart to bring your own brands of drugs, cosmetics, and the like, as the choices there may be limited.

All charter operations provide snorkeling equipment, and scuba gear can often be provided for qualified divers. Demanding experts may want to bring their own gear, but the average casual diver can be adequately equipped locally.

One Caribbean rule of thumb is that booze is cheap

and food is expensive. It's a waste of effort and money to bring your own liquor, although many visitors do the reverse and take liquor at bargain prices home with them. Some people bring down frozen steaks in a cooler, or perhaps some fancy hors d'oeuvres or other delicacies. But the provisioning by bareboat companies and crewed yachts is usually first-rate, and shopping in the local markets, while spotty and hit-or-miss on some things (depending on how recently a shipment has come in), usually takes care of at least the basic needs.

As for entertainment, your own Scrabble or Trivial Pursuit game might be a good idea, but most charter boats have a library of music tapes and a supply of reading material. If you have special tastes in reading, bring your own, but should you forget, paperbacks are generally available wherever there's shopping. The guide books and books of local interest listed in this book's bibliography make good ahead-of-time reading to make the area more interesting and meaningful.

Almost everyone brings a camera to the Caribbean, and the opportunities for photography are among the best anywhere. Although the more popular sizes of film used by tourists are generally available in the local shopping centers, and bigger cities have professional camera shops, it's advisable to bring your own film supply, as it's a nuisance to run out in an isolated area. In my experience, airport X-ray machines have not damaged film, but I do carry my unexposed film in a lead-lined bag—available at photo-supply stores—in my camera case.

If you're using a nonautomatic camera on which you have to set the exposure, the brightness of the tropic sun on the water and the reflection of light off the sea, sails, and deck can be hard to gauge. Usually it's wise

Getting There—and What to Bring

to cut down exposure one stop over what you're used to in similar northern situations.

A common fault in marine photography is to take scenes in which the subject is too far away. To take pictures of boats, a telephoto lens is recommended unless you're right alongside the subject, and many an eye-catching scene comes out flat and distant on film unless it is framed by something nearer.

As a general rule, don't try to have film developed in the islands unless you're in one of the bigger cities and staying awhile.

Fishing isn't a major activity in Caribbean sailing. There are sportfishing boats in many ports, and game fish are part of deep-water activity, but few charter yachts emphasize fishing. Routine fishing gear is available on most boats, but if you're an ardent angler, you might want to bring your own gear or inquire ahead of time as to what's available. In the northern Caribbean, the fish-poisoning disease known as ciguatera can be a problem. Ciguatera comes from the microscopic organisms eaten by reef-feeding fish, and can be transferred on up the food chain to game fish, and then to humans. Local fishermen seem to know where the fish are safe for consumption, but it's impossible for a visitor to be sure.

III

Chartering

Chartering in its various forms has become the major form of sailing in the Caribbean. In fact, on several islands, chartering has turned into an important local industry. Chartering started in the late Forties, when Commander V.E.B. Nicholson, a retired British naval officer, stopped with his family in Antigua aboard the ancient schooner *Mollihawk*. Nicholson and his family were supposedly on their way to a new postwar life in Australia, but as they rested and gathered forces in the deserted confines of English Harbour, ready to continue onward, they were asked to take guests from the Mill Reef Club, one of the Caribbean's first luxury, club-type resorts, for a daysail. Somehow, this seemed like a good business opportunity. They never left.

Commander Nicholson established the charter firm that still carries his name, and his sons, teenagers when they sailed on *Mollihawk,* now run the business. From this small beginning, chartering has grown into a big business. When we first chartered a Nicholson yacht out of Antigua in 1961, there were eleven yachts in the trade. Now there are hundreds and hundreds, spread around many harbors. Some forty to fifty thousand people a year come into the Caribbean to charter bareboats out of the British and American Virgins, many of the eastern Caribbean islands, and Belize and the Bay Islands in the western Caribbean. Charter boats dominate the scene in most harbors, although privately owned boats are also very much in evidence.

Bareboating, sailing without a professional crew aboard, is the principle form of chartering in terms of sheer numbers, but there are also hundreds of professionally crewed yachts operating out of St. Thomas, the British Virgins, Antigua, St. Martin, and the French islands.

Bareboat chartering started in St. Thomas, when Dick Avery, who ran a small marina and boatyard, persuaded some of his customers to put their boats out on charter early in the 1960s. By 1966 there were about a dozen boats available of various sizes and makes. Provisioning was the responsibility of the charterer. It was a very informal, loosely organized affair. Avery is still at it, but he's far from alone. A New Jersey dentist, Dr. Jack Van Ost, after chartering one of Avery's boats, saw the potential of a standardized fleet of bareboats. Using a package-tour approach to transportation and provisioning, he started Caribbean Sailing Yachts in St. Thomas. He soon moved his operation to the British Virgins, where a Louisiana couple, Charlie and Ginny Cary, had also seen the potential in bareboat chartering. The Carys started a company called The Moorings, which has grown into a major bareboat and resort operator in Tortola and St. Lucia.

Through the late Sixties and into the Seventies other firms followed the lead of these three, and there was a tremendous boom in new bareboat fleets and servicing facilities in the American and British Virgins. Most operated by selling boats to private owners on a lease-back arrangement, in which the charter company would operate the boats, with the owners amortizing them from charter fees while having the chance to use them a few weeks a year, usually on a tax-shelter basis. By the mid-Seventies, with hundreds of bareboats in operation, a whole new way of life had been established.

Meanwhile, the professionally crewed field had grown tremendously as well. In the early Nicholson days, the boats were a picturesque collection of old Brixham trawlers, Baltic traders, Alden schooners, and superannuated luxury yachts from before World War I. As competition increased, fancier and more sophisticated boats came into the trade, and today the bulk of professional charter yachts have been designed and built expressly for the purpose, with every conceivable amenity and modern convenience, top sailing performance, and high standards of "hotel-keeping" and gourmet cooking. Both forms of the charter industry have very definitely come of age.

The best way to get addresses for bareboat companies, brokers, and/or crewed charters is to look in the classified pages of national boating magazines.

Recommendations on Bareboating

While the boats available to charterers are of a wide range of sizes and types, there are some features and standardizations that have become widely accepted. The first thing to consider in a charter boat is the sleeping capacity. I don't mean to imply that this is the most important characteristic of the boat itself, but it does set the size range, so you should start from there in choosing boat size, having established the size of your group.

Many charters are on a cooperative basis, two or more couples splitting the cost. A boat may be advertised as a "seven-sleeper," but the charterer should relate the number of bunks to the size of the boat. There are boats under thirty feet that have six bunks, which may be all

Chartering

right for an ocean-racing crew or a single family, but it would be a mistake for three couples to take a boat of this size for a charter of a week or two. As a rule of thumb, I'd recommend that boats under thirty feet be for one couple (two couples only if they are young, adaptable, and good friends); thirty to forty feet for two couples; over forty feet for larger groups. More than three couples on a bareboat charter usually makes for friction and difficulties—in a group of this size there are almost always one or two people who are incompatible in the close quarters of a cruising auxiliary.

Choosing companions for a cruise should be done very carefully. We have certain friends we are completely sure of as cruising companions, and others who are delightful in certain circumstances but would not fit into life on board. Someone who is great fun at a Saturday night dance at the country club might not wear so well over a week of constant contact.

Most charter boats don't perform like Bermuda Race winners, to put it politely, although there has been a trend in recent years toward boats with a good performance factor. It's a rare sailor who is content to laze along being passed by everything in sight, so sailing qualities should be a priority of sorts.

Even more important, if the charter group is of both sexes, is the layout belowdecks. It's a real plus to have two private staterooms and two heads, which are easily available in boats over thirty-six feet. The privacy and convenience of these features cannot be overestimated in their effect on the success of a cruise. Even in boats in the forty-foot-and-up category, where there's room for three couples, one couple usually has to use the main cabin for sleeping and share one of the heads, so there is less privacy.

There are other amenities that should be considered.

The location of the galley, so that the cook isn't isolated from the rest of the group during "happy hour" and the like, is important. Ventilation is another, especially in the Caribbean. Are there enough hatches and opening ports? Space is also a consideration. Is the refrigerator capacity sufficient? Is there enough locker space to stow food, clothing, diving gear, and the like?

In the press of competition between bareboat operators, new touches of refinement are constantly being added. For instance, many bareboats now have built-in swimming ladders on the transom, ready for use at all times (incidentally, these are also a safety factor in man-overboard situations). Some boats have a deck shower right by the ladder for a quick rinsing of salt while away from the living areas.

Pressure hot water, mechanical refrigeration, VHF radio, depth sounder, speedometer, and electronic wind indicator—all are virtually standard equipment on fleet bareboats. There's little need for any other electronic navigation gear, such as Loran or Satnav, or for SSB radio. Elaborate nav stations, the pride and joy of so many private owners, aren't really needed aboard Caribbean bareboats.

The rig is a major feature. Ease of sailhandling and the adaptability of the rig to varying wind strengths are very important. Roller-furling jibs are almost universally in use on charter boats and are a wonderful convenience. Sail can be reduced rapidly from the cockpit and broken out just as easily. Few bareboat charterers like to do a lot of foredeck drill, changing jib sizes like an ocean-racing crew. Much simpler is the double headrig, with a roller-furling high-cut jib (sometimes called a Yankee) and a club-footed staysail. Along with jiffy-reefing on the mainsail, which, again, is almost universally in use, this is a versatile, flexible rig that can be adapted quickly to varying increases in wind strength with a minimum of fuss.

One problem with roller-furling jibs is getting them wound back onto the headstay in strong winds. The tension is sometimes so great that the early turns are too tight, and the whole sail can't be rolled up before the furling line is all the way off the drum. Putting the furling line on a winch helps greatly, but starting first turns can still be very difficult. If there's sea room, the best way to handle this problem is to head downwind until the mainsail is blanketing the jib. It's then much easier to get the turns started.

Quite a few bareboats have only one fairly large genoa-type jib, and the choices for reducing sail as the wind pipes up are very few with this rig. Roller-furling jibs can be used at half-furl in an emergency, but their shapes are usually ruined, and the center of effort goes the wrong way—higher and forward.

Roller-furling mainsails have come into use in some bareboat fleets, and they are a real convenience when it comes to dousing sail. The same considerations about reducing sail in a sudden, heavy increase of wind apply here, but without the ability to blanket the sail. Should the sail or mast get out of true, there can be a serious jam. Roller-furling mains come in several variations. One type goes into a slot in the mast and disappears. Another rolls up on a stay aft of and parallel to the mast, and a third type fits into a cloth sleeve on the after side of the mast. None is aerodynamically as good as the conventional main, and there always exists the possibility of a snafu. The compromise is between these negative factors and the obvious convenience in dousing sail.

In view of all these considerations, and after more than fifty years of cruising in every rig imaginable, I'd recommend a double headrig cutter with conventional main as the all-around best choice for a bareboat in the 36-to-40-foot range. In boats smaller than this, the split rig, universally a ketch now in bareboats, is inefficient, with too much clutter. The mizzen usually ruins the cockpit in an aft-cockpit boat, or hampers moving around in a center-cockpit one. In boats above 40 feet, the cutter rig is still very practical, but the divided rig can be handy in the increased opportunities for reducing sail in increments. When it's really blowing, the good old "jib and jigger" combination can be snug and easy.

Draft isn't an important consideration in Caribbean bareboating, as it would be in the Bahamas or along Florida's west coast, and the boats available are almost all monohulls. If the bareboat operators who have seventy to eighty boats in their fleets all had multihulls, their home-base pier facilities would have to be enormous, quite apart from many other space considerations. Multihull enthusiasts set on chartering that sort of boat would probably have to arrange to do it privately.

The big fleet operators don't offer boats under thirty feet, the economy range. There are marinas that have smaller boats of varying makes (this has been the case at Avery's, for instance, ever since his original pioneering in the field). But very few boats in this size range are designed with chartering in mind, unlike most of the boats in the fleet operations, and the criterion would simply be to pick a boat that suits your pocketbook and has adequate specifications.

Recommendations on Professionally Crewed Boats

In the professionally crewed field there's an extremely wide choice of boats, both sail and power. There's little standardization of facilities (as in the bareboat fleets,

Chartering

where the boats have all the individuality of motel rooms) and the method of operation is quite different. There's even a special kind of charter that concentrates completely on diving operations.

The professionally crewed boats are really floating hotel rooms. Guests are treated with all the attention that comes with staying at a luxury hotel, a treatment reflected in the prices. Whereas on bareboats the charterers have to do their own cooking as well as deck chores and sailhandling, on a professionally crewed yacht the guests don't have to raise a finger if they're not so inclined. Anyone who wants to can steer when they feel like it, and the guests can work the sails as much as they want to, but the business of serving drinks and meals (and the clean-up) is always handled by the crew.

There's no set standard for the makeup of crews on these yachts. In the smaller-size range, for example, boats are often handled by a husband-wife team, very often the owners of the boat, who handle everything. The wife is usually stewardess, deckhand, and cook, and the husband is skipper, navigator, mechanic, tour director, and "mine host" all rolled into one. Hence, anyone who doesn't like dealing with people would be sadly miscast working on a charter yacht. And since a charter season must usually run about twenty-six weeks in order to be profitable, there are a great many people to be dealt with.

But there are many variations on the husband-wife crew. Sometimes the cook-deckhand-strewardess is a young lady who has busted loose from conventional surroundings to seek adventure, and finds that the best way to earn a living while doing so is to get this sort of job. A large number of these young ladies, it seems, come to the Caribbean from Great Britain, but there's actually quite an international mix.

If the boat is a bit larger, in the sixty-foot-plus range, there will usually be a third person in the crew, either a deckhand or mechanic, or, treasure of treasures, one who serves as both. The well-run boat will be spotlessly clean at all times, gleaming with spit and polish, which means a constant round of maintenance chores.

The old-style charter boat that was the foundation for the business when it was getting started has all but disappeared. Just a few character vessels have kept going through the Eighties. Most of the boats are new and equipped with modern amenities. Some are even air conditioned (largely unnecessary in the Caribbean trade winds) and some new gimmicks are now almost standard, such as video-cameras that record a day's activities and are viewed that evening on the boat's TV, revealing to the guests just how they comported themselves.

Diving gear and high-powered tenders to take guests to good diving spots are also almost mandatory aboard crewed yachts, and many have Windsurfers and/or Sunfish for guests to use within the harbor. Needless to say, the galley department is usually of gourmet quality, and the outlay of meals, hors d'oeuvres, drinks, and snacks almost continuous.

Capacity standards for crewed boats are greater than for bareboat charters. Very few crewed boats are under forty feet, and those that are normally accommodate only one couple. Most are forty-five feet and up, and a two-couple limit is advisable until perhaps the mid-fifty-foot range (although much depends on the layout). A crewed yacht can be designed in a sensible fashion to accommodate more guests than a privately owned boat by doing away with one luxurious cabin and having cabins of equal space and comfort (this also avoids protocol problems among the guests over who gets the biggest cabin).

No matter what the physical setup of a boat, the success of a crewed charter ultimately rests on the personality of the professionals. If they manage to do things without apparent fuss and strain, keeping a cheerful face on everything, the battle is more than half won. It's a special knack, and the most successful operators have it and know how to use it.

How to Arrange a Bareboat Charter

What's the best way to set up a charter, either bareboat or crewed? How does the prospective charterer know that the foregoing recommendations are likely to be met in either type?

The two types of charter are handled quite differently. The bareboat fleets of standardized boats are operated in a routine manner out of set bases. The major ones have set up very businesslike booking procedures Stateside, and the whole charter can be packaged, there and back, by dealing with the charter company. The company handles air bookings, very often on a tour basis that's heavily discounted, plus ground transportation, provisioning, and nautical indoctrination. To be eligible to take on a bareboat charter, the charterer is supposed to provide some proof of competence in the form of a résumé of sailing background and, if possible, letters of recommendation. If there's some doubt about a charterer's qualifications, the charter company may put him through a checkout procedure at the charter base. If there's still doubt, the charterer may be required to take along, at extra expense, a professional seaman provided by the charter company. If someone has any hesitancy about his own qualifications, but would still like the lower cost and freedom of operation of a bareboat charter, it's a very good idea to sign up for this kind of arrangement. It's not as expensive as a crewed charter, and there's the security of having a knowledgeable professional aboard.

As explained elsewhere, I haven't included names and addresses, or prices, because these are so subject to change that they are often out of date by the time a book like this appears in print. The best up-to-date source of information on bareboat companies is in the charter advertising pages of the boating magazines, and all the major boating magazines put out a special charter issue at least once a year with a complete directory of companies.

Bareboat charter companies don't deal through the yacht brokerage firms that handle all other kinds of chartering and yacht sales, and that also advertise in the classified sections of boating magazines. The bareboat companies are their own agents and, as explained earlier, are equipped and eager to handle the whole transaction. Once they've established a charterer's qualifications, the company arranges specific dates and air travel, and also asks for requirements on food and liquor. Most companies have plans for complete or partial provisioning. Someone trying to save a penny may be able to shop at local markets, but in general the food provided by the charter companies is better than what's available locally, and the service is also a great convenience and time-saver.

The decision whether to provision fully or partially can be more than a pocketbook question. Eating ashore does add to the budget, but there's also the matter of the cook's morale. If one person does all the cooking, the trip won't be much of a vacation for that person.

Of course, the duties can be split among several people. And it's a good idea to keep meals as simple as possible, unless someone takes great pride in being a gourmet cook and revels in the opportunity.

In all bareboat areas there are pleasant places to eat ashore, and many of them can be an interesting adventure. It's often a rewarding experience to mingle with other yachting types at these shore spots. Trading sea stories and comparing notes can make for a stimulating evening. Credit cards are accepted in quite a few places, so the day of reckoning can be put off.

If the bareboat programs of the fleet operators don't appeal to you, it's possible to arrange individual charters of privately owned boats through yacht brokers, although this practice is much more prevalent in the continental United States than in the Caribbean. On rare occasions, there may be a hotshot ocean racer available between races for a performance-type cruise, and chartering smaller boats than the fleet operators provide can sometimes be done through brokers based in Caribbean yachting centers like St. Thomas, Tortola, St. Martin, or Antigua.

How to Arrange a Crewed Charter

Arranging for a crewed charter, sail or power, simple to luxurious, is done quite differently. As I've said, the bareboat companies will provide a paid hand on the boat if the charterer needs help, and some of their bigger boats do come with crew, but the individually operated crewed boats are mostly handled through established yacht brokers. Some boats place their own ads in magazines and handle direct inquiries, but most of the business is done through the brokers, whose ads appear in the rear pages of the boating magazines, and who are located in all parts of the country.

Most of the brokerage firms, whose main business is in selling used yachts, have one person in charge of their charter business as a separate, almost autonomous department. (In recent years, this has become an almost exclusively female province, with a very knowledgeable group of specialists, and there are several firms run by women that handle only charters.)

These agents have made it their business to become familiar with the industry on a worldwide basis; they know about Europe, the South Pacific, the continental United States, and the Greek islands. But the biggest percentage of their business is in the Caribbean. They do occasionally arrange individual bareboat charters of privately owned boats, but they mainly handle crewed boats. There's a distinct advantage in dealing with these charter brokers, because they are personally familiar with the boats they handle. Naturally, they can't cruise on all the hundreds of yachts they handle, but they do make an effort to cruise in the top areas every so often, so as to be familiar with the general situation.

Brokers get to know boats and the people who run them at annual charter boat shows. Boats gather at a central charter base sometime in the fall before the cruise season begins, and the brokers descend on them en masse for a concentrated session of boat-hopping and visiting. The Caribbean shows are held in St. Thomas, Road Town (Tortola), and Antigua. They take in the major fleets of crewed boats, and the brokers collect massive dossiers on everything, from the way the boats are set up to the personalities of the crews. They are then able to analyze what boat would suit a client's special requirements. These cruise brokers are like good travel agents who know the hotels and cruise ships they book, and their service is invaluable to the client who is merely feeling his way in the dark.

Boats that don't measure up to the scrutiny of these very professional brokers don't last long in the field; by the same token, brokers who don't know their stuff don't get return clients. So the whole system is of great benefit to the customer. In dealing with one of these brokers, the client should be as specific as possible about requirements, likes and dislikes, and, once the booking has been made, the special requirements for food and liquor.

And finally, the brokerage fee is paid as a commission by the yacht, not the customer, so it can be economically worthwhile as well to arrange a charter booking in this manner.

Owning a Charter Boat

Most of the bareboat fleets are set up so that its boats are sold to individuals and then leased back to the fleet operator, who manages completely the charter bookings and boat maintenance for a specified number of years. Charter payments are used to amortize the purchase of the boat, and, in many cases, the arrangement can be set up as a tax shelter. While the boat is on lease-back, the owner gets to use her for free for a period of two to three weeks, usually in the off season, but must pay the charter rate if he wants to use her in season. At the end of the lease-back period, the owner has paid for the boat (and might even have a profit) and has the boat to sell or to use according to his needs. Each company has its variations, which couldn't all be explained in detail in the scope of this book. But that's the general economic scheme.

In the crewed boat field there are many different arrangements. Some boats are owner-operated, while others are owned by "absentee landlords," either corporations or individuals, and run by professional crews. In the Caribbean there exists an international setup, boats owned in many countries. Some base there all year, while others are shuttled to the Mediterranean or the U.S. Northeast for the summer.

No matter what the type of business, chartering is the single biggest element in the growth of yachting in the Caribbean, the means whereby thousands of people enjoy its delights when they otherwise would never have been able to. Chartering has certainly come a long way since Commander Nicholson first brought *Mollihawk* into English Harbour.

IV

Operating a Private Boat

Although chartering encompasses the majority of those cruising in the Caribbean, there's a goodly number of private boats as well. In such centers as Puerto Rico, St. Thomas, Tortola, St. Martin, Antigua, and the French islands, sizable numbers of boats owned by permanent residents are at yacht clubs and marinas. Increasingly, boats owned by Americans, Canadians, and Europeans are being based in the islands year-round. Some are retirement boats—floating homes inhabited full time, while others are used for part-time vacations. Some are available for charter through Stateside and/or Caribbean brokers. In addition, there is the usual peripatetic population of passage boats, world voyagers on their way through on a circumnavigation, Atlantic circle, or Caribbean cruise.

We've based our CSY 37, *Brunelle*, in the British Virgin Islands since taking her there in the spring of 1979, and have found that, while there are special considerations and conditions, it's not a difficult thing to do. It's no more expensive than maintaining a boat in a northern marina or boatyard (our main extra expense is "commuting" to her). In a typical year, we spend a total of about five months on her. On our trips home to tend to business, finances, and meetings, she stays in wet storage at Village Key Marina in Road Town, Tortola. She's tended by a professional boatkeeping service that opens her up for ventilation periodically, turns over the engine to keep it in working order and to charge the batteries, and does routine maintenance work of all sorts at labor rates that are better than Stateside ones. The standard of workmanship is perfectly satisfactory. The service's monthly fees depend on a boat's size (fifty-five dollars in *Brunelle*'s case).

Most major centers have services like this and also boatyards for haulouts and any major work that might need to be done. *Brunelle* has been hauled each November at Tortola Yacht Services for waxing and bottom painting prior to our first visit of the season. The antifouling lasts well enough until May, when we leave her for the summer.

The biggest inconvenience is in getting spare parts. There are chandleries in most centers, but major items, such as replacements for toilets and hot-water tanks, which we eventually needed, came from the States and were slow in arriving (as well as subject to duties). Routine items like new fenders, dock lines, batteries, tools, paints, charts, tape, glue, and the hundreds of little items that make up the greatest part of ships' stores are generally available. There are sail lofts for new sails and repairs. (We had a very inexpensive repair done on our staysail by a furniture upholsterer in St. Martin, and a serviceable replacement for the Bimini top was made in Road Town after six seasons of use. Road Town, as an example, has good mechanics, refrigeration men, electricians, and riggers, and the same can be said of most of the other areas.)

There is red tape to consider. Regulations vary in each island as to length of stay allowed exempt from duties, cruising fees, requirements for entering and clearing, and customs. The Dutch side of St. Martin, for example, has no customs at all, while most of the islands do, with varying degrees of strictness (in most of them, the

Operating a Private Boat

banging of rubber stamps is a major local industry). In places like Cruz Bay, St. John, Fort de France, Martinique, Marigot Bay, St. Lucia, St. George's, Grenada, and English Harbour on Antigua, customs offices have been set up specifically for yachts and are relatively convenient.

All-weather security is an important consideration. A boat in off-season lay-up must be in a hurricane-proof location, and there aren't many harbors that combine the dockage space and landlocked protection that this requires. Eastern Puerto Rico, in the Fajardo area, has several marinas that fill the bill, and The Lagoon on St. Thomas does as well. In the British Virgins, the Wickham's Cay complex at the head of Road Town Harbour, protected by a man-made seawall, is secure, as are Nanny Cay Marina, three miles to the west, and Virgin Gorda Yacht Harbour on Virgin Gorda. Dry storage is provided by Tortola Yacht Services and Virgin Gorda. Simson Lagoon, St. Martin, and English Harbour and Parham Sound, Antigua, are completely protected, as are a couple of marinas on Guadeloupe. Marigot Bay, St. Lucia, and The Lagoon at St. George, Grenada, are other harbors where a boat may be safely left in wet storage.

Aside from protection from the weather, security from thievery is important, and the British Virgin Islands spots seem to be among the best for this. In all areas, it's asking for trouble to leave a boat completely untended and therefore important to have a boatkeeper of some sort, such as an individual, the dock crew at the marina, or a professional boat-tending service.

Brunelle has weathered two hurricanes in the Virgin Islands. In one she was in dry storage at Tortola Yacht Services, and in the other she was in a slip at Village Cay Marina, Wickham's Cay. The dockmaster, friends on neighboring boats, and the boatkeeping service combined to make sure that her lines and fenders were all right, but she would have broken some lines from the surge and been in trouble if no one had looked after her. (She was in stripped condition for the lay-up, with sails off the spars and the Bimini and all loose deck gear stowed.)

A boat kept in the tropics all the time undergoes ravages from the hot, direct sun. Topsides brightwork must be attended to almost continuously, sail covers must be used whenever there's even a day or two of layover, and the effect is severe on items like Bimini tops. Teak dries out and goes gray, and should be treated periodically. Instrument dials, if exposed to direct sun for any length of time, tend to warp and discolor. (We protect ours with aluminum foil.) The same is true of compasses, which should always be kept covered when not in use.

Another fact of tropical life is the cockroach. As careful as you might be in removing cardboard shopping cartons as soon as they're unloaded, and as clean as you keep a boat, cockroaches do get aboard, especially when the boat is alongside a pier for any length of time. Periodic fumigation is a must.

What kind of dinghy to have is an important decision. Charter boats all have dinghies that are ruggedly built and specially designed for easy towing, but they're too big to be brought aboard as a routine matter and must be towed all the time. If you're concerned with sailing performance, towing can be a nuisance. On the other hand, it can be just as big a nuisance hauling a tender on and off the deck. Our compromise has been an inflatable eight-foot Avon, which is light enough for me to launch and recover by myself, and can be stowed easily on deck. We've managed to do without outboard power, partially because we have no deck aft of the cockpit and therefore no convenient place to stow an outboard, and partially because I really don't want to keep gasoline aboard. On certain occasions, it might have been helpful to take a long dinghy trip across a harbor rather than hire a cab, but in general we're happy with our compromise.

Racing

One of the advantages of having your own boat in the Caribbean, if you are so inclined, is the proliferation of racing in recent years. There are several events that are as hotly contested and as serious in the quality of competition as similar events in the States, like the Southern Ocean Racing Conference (SORC). There are races for locally based fleets in most of the active centers, like Puerto Rico, St. Thomas, Tortola, St. Martin, Antigua, the French islands, and the Grenadines. There's also the Caribbean Ocean Racing Conference, modeled on SORC, that's made up of regattas in Puerto Rico—the Copa Velasco, the Rolex Regatta in St. Thomas, and the B.V.I. Spring Regatta. Antigua Race Week is a separate event now. These events were started as rather casual local affairs, but they've grown into seriously contested racing series, attracting yachts from all over the Caribbean, North America, Europe, and even Australia. They somehow symbolize the increased sophistication of the yachting scene in recent years.

V

The Islands Profiled

From a sailor's point of view, each of the islands of the Caribbean has a separate personality, and what they offer the visiting yachtsman also varies dramatically from island to island. As explained in the Preface, this book is not intended as the type of cruising guide with specific instructions to be followed, chart in hand, while entering a harbor. The regularly updated guides listed in the Bibliography are the best way to keep up with that information. Here, we're concerned with the general aspects of each island and what it offers to the visiting sailor.

The Greater Antilles west of Puerto Rico are not covered here, since they don't offer charter opportunities, and private boats visiting them should make use of the updated cruising guides. In any case, it's important to plan ahead and to consult with diplomatic authorities on current political conditions before venturing to Haiti and the Dominican Republic. Jamaica is off the beaten track, and, at this writing, Cuba is a no-man's-land for yachtsmen. Too bad, because Cuba offers wonderful cruising opportunities on both its north and south coasts. Maybe someday . . .

The only areas of the western Caribbean of interest to yachtsmen at present are the Bay Islands in the Bay of Honduras, the Belize Reef, and, to a lesser extent, the islands off Venezuela and the San Blas Islands of Panama.

The Islands Profiled

Puerto Rico

Puerto Rico is self-governing, in association with the United States, with all of the advantages of this association (as well as the disadvantages of crowding and commercialization). An American yacht isn't in foreign waters here but must clear customs and immigration when entering from a non-American island. Many Puerto Ricans own boats, and it's perhaps the only Caribbean area where motorboats at least equal the number of sailboats in the local fleet. The major yachting center is the Fajardo area at the northeast corner of the island. There are several large marinas with perfect protection on the main island near the town of Fajardo, and a major marina and service yard in Isleta Marina, less than half a mile off the coast. San Juan is no longer an important yachting base, although it does have facilities tucked away at the eastern end of its big harbor. The open Atlantic outside is usually rough, and there's a considerable distance to travel to the most attractive boating waters.

The north coast of Puerto Rico isn't set up well for pleasure boating, as there are almost no harbors on this exposed shore. Arecibo, near the western end, has protection but few facilities. Any cruising out of Puerto Rico is done along the south coast, where there are several good harbors, such as Palmas del Mar, Bahia de Jobos, Salinas, Caja de Murtos, Ponce—a sizable city with a yacht club—and Parguera, famous for its phosphorescence. Off the east coast, the islands of Vieques and Culebra have several good harbors. Vieques is taken up in large part by military operations, as is Roosevelt Roads, the big U.S. naval base on the east end of the main island, but Culebra, which used to be a bombing range, is now free of military operations and has an excellent hurricane hole in the many coves of Ensenada Honda. It also has attractive off-lying islets, several fine beaches, and good snorkeling and diving.

Puerto Rico is off the track for charter operations, and the activity there is in private boats. As an island, it's not as scenic as those farther south, but the breeze, the sun, and the water colors are all there.

The U.S. Virgin Islands

St. Thomas, overtouristed, crowded, and one of the world's busiest cruise ship ports, is base for a great many bareboats, crewed charters, and private boats. With a newly expanded jet airport at Charlotte Amalie, and steep hills so top-heavy with development that it looks as though the place might capsize, St. Thomas is an island to cruise *from*, not *to*.

The various corners of Charlotte Amalie Harbor are jammed with yachts, and Yacht Haven Marina at the east end is the biggest installation. The Lagoon, halfway down the southern shore to the eastward, is another busy base, though quite shallow, and Red Hook, around the corner on the east coast, is another harbor full of service facilities, despite its being open to the prevailing easterlies. Cowpet Bay, at the southeast corner, is the location of the very active St. Thomas Yacht Club. There are few cruising harbors per se, as everyone heads eastward as soon as he is ready to sail. Christmas Cove, opposite Cowpet Bay on St. James Island, is a popular stop on the way east, and Magens Bay is about the only good anchorage on the north coast.

St. John, the smallest of the U.S. Virgins, is ringed with lovely harbors. Cruz Bay, three miles from Red Hook, is a port of entry without much room for visitors, but Caneel Bay, Trunk Bay, Francis Bay, and

Leinster Bay on the north coast of St. John are all fine, picturesque anchorages. Hurricane Hole, a deep indentation in St. John's eastern coast, has several good spots, and the south coast has Salt Pond, Lameshur, Rendezvous, Great Cruz Bays, and Chocolate Hole. All these are open anchorages in the rare event of a southerly. Much of St. John has been designated as a national park, and as a result the island is relatively empty, with camping the main tourist activity.

St. Croix, off by itself thirty miles to the south, is the largest of the U.S. Virgins. It's not a charter center or popular target for visiting private boats, although there's plenty of boating activity out of Christiansted, its only well-protected harbor.

The U.S. Virgins, purchased from Denmark in 1917, still retain many Danish place names, and, an anomaly in U.S. territories, driving on the left-hand side of the road. (First-time visitors, not aware of this driving practice, gasp in astonishment during their first taxi ride.)

The British Virgin Islands

Starting just a mile away from St. John across a current-swept strait called The Narrows, the British Virgins cover a relatively small area of not more than one hundred square miles between the western end of Tortola and Virgin Gorda, twenty miles to the eastward. This area doesn't include Anegada, a low, sandy, reef-girt island twenty miles north of Virgin Gorda. Anegada is off-limits to bareboats because of its surrounding reefs. Despite the compact area, the B.V.I. (as they are usually referred to) have become the bareboat capital of the world, as well as base for many crewed charter boats and a sizable fleet of private boats.

Tortola is the largest island, seventeen miles long, with the highest peak in all the Virgins, Mt. Sage, just under eighteen hundred feet. Tortola forms one side of the heart of Virgin Island sailing, Sir Francis Drake Channel, which lies on the east-west axis between The Narrows and Virgin Gorda. The south side of the three-mile-wide channel is enclosed by a string of smaller islands: Norman, Peter, Dead Chest, Salt, Cooper, Ginger, and Fallen Jerusalem. The other major island is Jost Van Dyke (named for a Dutch pirate of old), west of Tortola.

The British Virgins, a rather small expanse of land and water, manage to combine all the ingredients of ideal cruising. There are more than thirty anchorages (though some of them are only for lunch stops, like the Baths on Virgin Gorda). All have reliable breezes, beautiful, mostly well-protected water, and graceful scenery. In addition, recent years have seen the development of first-rate marinas and haulout yards. There's nowhere else in the world that I know of that's better set up for pleasant, relaxed cruising in beautiful surroundings.

Since the B.V.I. are a British colony, entering and clearing formalities must be gone through in moving between them and the U.S.V.I. West End and Road Town, Tortola, Great Harbour on Jost Van Dyke, and Virgin Gorda Yacht Harbour are ports of entry. Road Town, on a wide bay midway along the south shore of Tortola, is the capital and major town, with several marinas, a big service yard, shops, markets, restaurants, and hotels. The B.V.I. don't have any high-rises or big hotels. All hotels are of modest size, and most are of the out-island club type. Up until 1970, Road Town was a sleepy village with no shoreside facilities, a few local fishing boats and island freighters, and an occasional visiting yacht. Today, the bay is ringed by a forest of aluminum masts, and the anchorages are full. But there's still a relaxed, low-key atmosphere.

The major marinas are at Road Town, Nanny Cay, and Virgin Gorda Yacht Harbour, and the major cruising attraction is Gorda Sound, a landlocked bay on the northeast side of Virgin Gorda. Smart planning for a B.V.I. cruise should call for a beat eastward to Gorda Sound in the first day or two; after that it's all downwind through a choice of thirty or so harbors, back to the charter bases of Road Town, Nanny Cay, or St. Thomas.

St. Maarten-St. Martin

From the compact charms of the Virgin Islands there's a considerable change of conditions as you proceed down the arc of islands stretching almost five hundred miles to just off the South American mainland. From Virgin Gorda, it's eighty miles dead to windward to the next island in the arc, the Dutch-French, dual-nation St. Maarten-St. Martin (hereinafter St. Martin) across Anegada Passage. In this passage, weather systems and currents from the North American continent, the Caribbean, and the Atlantic all meet and clash in a turbulent, unpredictable mix. What *is* predictable is that the seas will be confused and sloppy, with no distinct pattern, and the weather will change almost without warning from benign to squally. This disturbed and disturbing stretch is about as unpopular with yachtsmen as a body of water can be. (In our family it's been nicknamed "O-My-Gawd-Ah" Passage.) Some people say they've had quiet crossings of the passage, but it's never happened in my experience, and the opinion I've sampled is virtually unanimous: this is a nasty, rugged place, to be gotten through as quickly as possible. Bareboats don't make the crossing, but some crewed charters do.

St. Martin has had its dual nationality for several centuries in peace, no matter what was going on in Europe. The division was supposedly established by having a Frenchman and a Dutchman depart from a single starting place and walk around the island in opposite directions. The other end of the boundary was where they met. It's a good story, but there are many stretches of St. Martin's coastline where it would be impossible to walk. In any event, the island is a fascinating example of national characteristics. The Dutch half is now a thoroughly Americanized, highly developed resort, while the French side is simply very French.

St. Martin is a late bloomer on the yachting scene, but it has been catching up fast. In the early days of development, with the Virgins and Antigua as major charter bases, St. Martin was a no-man's-land in the middle with no facilities to speak of. Because it was a tough beat from the Virgins, and almost as tough a beat to get back to Antigua from this area, few boats ventured there. Since the late Seventies, however, it has been "discovered," and, despite a lack of good all-weather harbors, it's now the base for many bareboats, crewed charters, and private boats. In season, Philipsburg, the Dutch capital, has over a hundred boats in its broad, shallow, surgy bay.

In addition to having Anguilla and St. Barts as nearby attractions, St. Martin has several attractive harbors of its own. While Philipsburg can be uncomfortable in a surge, it's where the action is in the way of marinas, shopping, casinos, nightlife, and transportation. Simson Bay, Marigot, Grand Case, Marcel Bay, and Orient Bay, with its separate anchorages at Ile Pinel and Green Cay, are all good spots in the right weather (all have at least one open exposure), and Oyster Pond, though owning a narrow entrance giving right into the open Atlantic to the east, is a beautifully snug harbor.

An untapped potential on St. Martin is sizable Simson Lagoon, which is completely landlocked and takes up much of the western half of the island. It has only been accessible through infrequently opened drawbridges, and isn't practical for daily use, but it's a perfect hurricane hole, much used in that season by boats permanently moored in St. Martin. A more easily operated drawbridge was installed in 1985, and may make the lagoon more accessible to transients.

St. Martin has direct jet connections with New York, Miami, several other U.S. airports, and cities in Europe. Consequently, it has all the attractions (and some drawbacks) of a highly developed resort.

Anguilla

Six miles north of St. Martin, Anguilla is the northernmost of the Lesser Antilles. Except for the tiny outpost of Sombrero Island, with its powerful lighthouse in the middle of Anegada Passage, there's no more land in that direction until Africa or Europe. Anguilla is small (about sixteen miles long) and narrow, which prompted Columbus to give it the Spanish name for eel. Its highest hill is only about three hundred feet, but it makes up for lack of mountain scenery with some of the most gorgeous, untouched beaches in the West Indies.

With its six thousand or so inhabitants—mostly small farmers, salt producers, and fishermen—Anguilla slumbered in obscurity for centuries until it was thrust into the spotlight via a bizarre series of events in the Sixties. Unhappy with being the poor relation in the Associated State of St. Kitts-Nevis-Anguilla, Anguillans wanted out, preferring to go back to the status of a

British colony. Before everything was straightened out there were such comic opera doings as an "invasion" by British paratroopers and London bobbies (in full winter uniforms) and all sorts of misunderstandings. Finally, however, the British became convinced of the true Anguillan intentions, and Anguilla was accepted back into what was left of the British Empire.

After this spate of publicity, Anguilla settled back into its peaceful mode of living, only to be caught up gradually in the explosion of yachting activity out of St. Martin and the expansion of tourism. By the mid-Eighties, the island had been "discovered" by travel writers. A couple of luxury resorts, modest in size but top-notch in facilities and style, were added to the simple guest-house and out-island-club type of accommodations that had been available. New restaurants opened, and the harbors began to see more and more yachts. Road Bay on the north coast is the main yachting harbor and port of entry.

There have been problems with customs procedures, cruising permits, and port fees in Anguilla, with a fairly steep charge per day for cruising permits, although efforts were being made to alleviate the situation when I last checked. If a visiting yacht is given permission, there are a number of spots worth visiting, such as Sandy Island just outside Road Bay, and the Prickly Pear Cays a bit farther off. These should be strictly lunch stops. Boats venturing to stay at the Prickly Pears overnight can be caught in a heavy surge, which can develop suddenly at this outpost on the edge of the Atlantic. Crocus Bay on the north coast and Rendezvous Bay on the south are attractive anchorages with good beaches. Island Harbour and isolated Scrub Island at the eastern end are other anchorages, and the south coast offers one or two roadstead-type bays.

Dog Island, ten miles northwest of Road Bay, is an intriguing spot, but its status has varied over the years and it is sometimes off-limits, so it's best to check with the authorities before venturing out there.

St. Barthélemy (St. Barts)

On the other side of St. Martin is the distinctive island of St. Barthélemy. Named by Columbus for his brother, it's now universally referred to by its short name, St. Barts. About a dozen miles southeast of St. Martin, it has only a couple of good anchorages, but it stands so much alone in contrasting atmosphere and lifestyle to all other Caribbean islands that it has become a very popular stop. All this has developed since the mid-Seventies, when guide books described it as a secret hideaway, a haven for smugglers where visiting yachts were rare. By the mid-Eighties its main port, Gustavia, had become one of the most crowded harbors in all the islands.

Small (about six by three miles), steeply hilly but not mountainous, ringed with good beaches, St. Barts is French, in fact very French, and also in reverse racial proportion to all other West Indian islands, as its population of twenty-five hundred is 90 percent white. Although it's been French since the middle of the seventeenth century, when it was first settled, Sweden ruled it from 1784 to 1878 in one of those political swaps European rulers were wont to make. This rule is memorialized in the name Gustavia and in its Swedish street names.

Tourism has replaced smuggling as the main industry on St. Barts. Tiny STOL planes drop down to its minuscule airport at a steep angle in a steady stream bringing in visitors; yachts also bring many tourists.

Gustavia has gone from being a deserted smuggler's haven to a bustling port with a hundred or more boats bobbing outside in the roadstead or squeezed into the tiny inner harbor. Here, the drill is to anchor fore and aft in the center of the harbor if there's room, or to find a spot along the seawalls and anchor in Mediterranean fashion.

Once the most informal of ports, where French-speaking young ladies in the customs office up the hill from the harbor would giggle in confusion at someone trying to enter in a yacht, the harbor is now very organized. A port officer in a Boston Whaler checks boats in as they arrive, and entry is then effected at a port office on the quay in the inner harbor. This is done very efficiently, with a small port charge for simultaneous entry and clearance.

There are a few calm-weather harbors on the Atlantic side of St. Barts, such as Baie de Saint Jean, but the only other generally usable anchorage beside Gustavia, which is almost perpetually surgy in the outer harbor, is Baie Colombier at the northwest tip. It's a pretty spot, well-protected unless a surge moves in from the north. There's an exceptionally nice beach at its inner end, and the point that encloses it on the west side is known as Rockefeller Point, as the sprawling house atop the hill to the west has been the Caribbean hideaway of David Rockefeller.

A mile or two west of Baie Colombier, the deserted island of Ile Fourche, with its highly visible four peaks, has a pleasant and well-protected harbor indenting its center.

Saba

Each Caribbean island has certain unique features, but Saba differs from them all—physically, socially, and nautically. About twenty-five miles southwest of St. Martin, Saba's volcanic cone makes a dramatic silhouette on the horizon, and the drama is heightened on closer approach. The peak is just under three thousand feet high, and the island is almost as round as a dollar, with the only indentation a windward-side bay at the northeast quadrant. The point on the north side of this little bay is practically the only flat spot on Saba, and a STOL airstrip that looks about half the size of a football field as you approach has been fashioned there. Built in 1963, it has made a great difference in how visitors and supplies get ashore on Saba.

For centuries, the only access to Saba's steep slopes was through the surf at Fort Bay, a tiny curve in the shoreline to the southwest, with a very small pebbly beach. Everything that came ashore, no matter how bulky, had to be brought in by surfboat and carried up the hills to the settlements in the center of the island by porter or donkey.

An ambitious road-building program that started in the Fifties and took twenty years to complete opened up the island to motor vehicles. The final step in improving access was a 277-foot stone and concrete pier built in 1972 at Fort Bay. Since the bottom drops away very steeply from Saba's shores, this pier was an engineering feat in itself. The pier encloses a small basin that is all right in calm weather but subject to severe surge when the weather is rough. There are a couple of moorings just offshore, and an anchorage of sorts exists around to the west at Ladder Bay, where one must climb five hundred steps to get to the nearest road.

Saba has been Dutch since the game of military and political musical chairs between European powers cooled off early in the nineteenth century, but its language is English. The population of a couple of thousand is split equally between black and white and is located in three settlements: The Bottom, Windward Side, and Hell's Gate. By comparison to the litter and clutter amid run-down shacks on most Caribbean islands, the settlements are incredibly neat, in typical Dutch fashion, with red-roofed white houses all painted every two years and garden plots carefully tended. There's a perpetual roller-coaster feeling on Saba, as you are always going up or down, and breathtaking views of the sea and the other islands suddenly appear around a bend or over the crest of a hill.

We have only visited the island itself by plane, but *Brunelle* has been in the basin once with a family crew aboard. Whatever the nautical difficulties, Saba is very much worth a visit.

St. Eustatius (Statia)

Statia is eighteen miles below Saba down the southeastward arc of islands. It has very little to offer yachtsmen, as the harbor is an open roadstead and very rolly, and there isn't much to see or buy on the island. Its claim to fame for Americans is as the first place the flag of the new republic received official recognition, when the fort of Oranjestad fired a salute for the American frigate *Andrew Doria* in November 1776. At the time, this was one of the busiest ports in the Caribbean and an important staging point for war matériel being sent to the States. Before long, Admiral Rodney brought his British fleet up from St. Lucia and completely ransacked the piers and storehouses, carrying off a great amount of booty. Statia, it seems, has never recovered, and is almost a ghost island today, except for some farming and a few guest houses. With a dramatic pile of clouds building over its anvil-shaped peak, it does make a handsome profile for passing boats.

St. Christopher (St. Kitts)

The next island down the chain is one of the handsomest to look at when ranging its leeward coast, which is dominated by the ruins of an old fort on Brimstone Hill and a number of towering peaks, topped by 4,314-foot Mt. Misery, the highest in this part of the Caribbean. Bright green sugar fields are draped across the lower slopes almost up to the virtually permanent cloud cover. St. Kitts, as this island is always called, is the oldest settlement in the Lesser Antilles, and one of the few still based on a sugar economy. It too has very little for the cruising sailor. There's a windy, rolly, open roadstead at Basseterre, the capital, and a few coves on the low tail of the island at its southeast end. Over the years, St. Kitts has had a bad reputation for its handling of customs and immigration for yachts. There's one horror story of a large powerboat that had an expensive stereo set stolen while at anchor there. When the owner reported the theft to the police, not only were they of no help in locating it, they also told him he was liable for duty because the equipment had been "imported" into St. Kitts. That was a few years ago, but it's still important to find out ahead of time what the current political climate is. Or to go on.

Nevis

The next island is St. Kitts's sister island, Nevis, two miles across The Narrows, a reef-strewn strait. The main town here is Charlestown, which is also the only anchorage.

It's an open roadstead on a curve of beach protected from the southeast by a low point with the ruins of Fort Charles at the end of it. Nevis was named by Columbus for the perpetual "snowcap" of clouds on its symmetrical peak. It's a quiet, much more low-key island than St. Kitts, with a slower pace and friendlier people. There are a few pleasant inns and guest houses on the slopes of the hill, and Charlestown still looks like the Caribbean ports of old.

Montserrat

This is another island with little to offer the cruising sailor, because it has no real harbor. Montserrat is mountainous, scenic, rich in agriculture and in local color, but Plymouth, the capital, is a rolly, open roadstead. The only possible protection is in Cars Bay at the northwest tip, though I've had reports of a bad surge there, too. This is too bad, because Montserrat is strategically located thirty-five miles southeast of Nevis, thirty-five miles northwest of Guadeloupe, and thirty-five miles southwest of Antigua, and would be a good stopover on passages between them. Montserrat's main interest for cruising yachts is Radio Antilles, a powerful AM station that covers the entire eastern Caribbean and gives weather reports at 0650, 0805, 1235, and 1830 hours. The reports are a bit general ("Winds will be northeast to southeast, ten to twenty-six knots" is typical), but they do advise of any unusual weather conditions.

Halfway down the rhumb line between Montserrat and Nevis is the 750-foot rock pinnacle of Redonda, a sheer peak that looks uninhabitable but has been home for phosphate-mining operations in the past. In 1911, Frederic Fenger, a pioneer long-voyager who made a

Grenada–Virgin Islands passage in the little sailing canoe *Yakaboo*, spent a night there at the house of the mining superintendent, getting there by being hoisted four hundred feet up the cliff face in a phosphate basket while his canoe sat at a steamship buoy. When sailing by the peak's rugged silhouette, however, it's hard to imagine that it has ever been anything but deserted.

Antigua/Barbuda

One of the newest independent nations in the Caribbean is this two-island country at the "elbow" of the Lesser Antilles, where the string of islands finally turns from its southeastward arc to a direct north-south axis. Antigua has long been the major yachting center of the central Lesser Antilles, and is still very much so, despite the development of the other islands. It is, as previously pointed out, where chartering started in the Caribbean, with English Harbour as a base. The dockyard at English Harbour, where Lord Nelson based the British fleet in North American colonial times, was a jumble of ruins when *Mollihawk* made her landfall there, but it wasn't hard to imagine what it had been like in Nelson's day.

Over the years, the dockyard has gradually been restored. Today all the buildings are back in use in some fashion, but they still reek with atmosphere and form the basis for an unusual yachting facility. Old cannon are upended in the lawn as bollards, and careening winches have been preserved. The seawall, surrounding the circular point on which the buildings sit, is much the same as it was originally, and is now perpetually jammed with yachts moored stern-to (Mediterranean fashion) on a first-come first-served basis. English Harbour's narrow entrance, hard to detect from offshore, provides the perfect protection that was important to the British fleet; it was easy to defend from forts on the high surrounding hills. Military aspects are no longer of importance, but the protection from bad weather is as good as in any Caribbean port.

If the seawall is fully occupied, there's anchoring room outside the dockyard in Freeman Bay and to a lesser extent in the inner harbor. Many boats are left here in wet storage, tied securely to mangroves along the eastern side. There's a full-service slipway capable of handling large yachts up to 150 tons and 120 feet length over all on the east side.

Due to the tremendous pressure put on English Harbour by the growth in yachting activity, harbors in nearby bays have also been developed. Just to the west, spacious Falmouth Harbour, boasting a pier with fuel and fresh water, offers good protection and is cooler and breezier than English Harbour. (It's even possible to swim here.) Falmouth is the site of the active Antigua Yacht Club.

Falmouth Harbour isn't a port of entry, but English Harbour is. There, formalities are strictly observed, and yachts must wait in the quarantine anchorage in Freeman Bay until cleared. In both English and Falmouth Harbours, nominal anchoring fees are charged.

Three miles east of English Harbour is the luxurious St. James's Club, opened in 1984. As well as a first-class hotel with a casino, several restaurants, horseback riding, tennis, and water sports on windward and leeward beaches, it is now a port of entry, a great convenience in avoiding the hassle at Freeman Bay. It has anchoring room and moorings for a big fleet, as well as space at its marina pier for about thirty yachts on Mediterranean moors. Fuel, water, electricity, and ice are available, as well as sportfishing charters and dive expeditions. Participation is on a club basis, and visiting yachtsmen can obtain temporary membership for a modest fee.

Another recent development is Crabbs Marina on Parham Sound at the northeast tip of Antigua, far removed from south coast installations. It too is a full-service marina with modest rooms available ashore, plus a restaurant and chandlery, repairs, haulout, and a bareboat fleet.

Antigua is one of the few islands in the Lesser Antilles where a one-island cruise is possible. There are good anchorages (unless a rare westerly surge is present) on the west side at Five Islands, Mosquito Cove, Deep Bay, and Dickenson Bay. St. Johns, the capital, though dirty and commercialized, has good protection and a harborside market. Parham Sound has some pleasant coves; Green Island on the east coast is one of the nicest anchorages; and Carlisle Bay and Curtain Bluff on the south coast are good lunch stops as well as overnight anchorages if the wind isn't south of east.

Barbuda, where the only facility, Coco Point Hotel, did not at last report welcome yachtsmen, has other isolated anchorages at Gravenor Bay, Palmetto Point, and Spanish Point, with some of the best beaches and diving to be found anywhere. Barbuda, twenty-five miles north of Antigua, is completely flat and surrounded by reefs. It's almost always a reach there and back, but navigation must be done very carefully, eyeballing in good light.

Guadeloupe

Guadeloupe, the big, mountainous island forty miles south of Antigua, is a department of France, and as such is well developed and quite civilized, especially around its main city, Point-à-Pitre. Shaped like a butterfly, with a narrow neck connecting the two "wings," Guadeloupe has harbors on both halves, and many locally based boats, both private and charter. Point-à-Pitre, located on the eastern wing, Grande-Terre, is a noisy, busy commercial harbor, though a modern marina has been established nearby. There are good restaurants in the area and direct air service to the U.S. and Europe from its jetport.

There are several interesting coves on the bay that separates the two halves of Guadeloupe, and a new marina at Passe Champagne. Yachts making the north-south passage between Antigua and points south seldom come around to this area, instead using the west coast as a stopover, but anyone chartering out of Point-à-Pitre would find a good choice of harbors.

The western wing of the island is called Basse-Terre; the most reliable anchorage there is DesHayes (spelled DesHaies on some charts), forty-two miles from English Harbour on what is almost invariably a fast reach. DesHayes, a quiet Caribbean village with no tourist influences, offers good protection and holding ground. This area of the coast, incidentally, is infested with fish pots, and a good eye must be kept open for them at all times. For this reason, a night passage along the coast of Guadeloupe is not recommended. Anyone wishing to make a night passage should stay at least five miles off to the west (where the breeze should be more reliable anyway). Very often, in normal trade-wind weather, there's a fresh westerly backwind close under the leeward shore of Guadeloupe.

There are possible anchorages at Pigeon and Anse à la Barque, and a new marina south of the city of Basse-Terre, the capital of Guadeloupe, at the Sens River, has made this area more attractive for stopping—although the marina may be completely full of local boats.

Les Iles des Saintes

"The Saints," as English-speaking visitors refer to them, are politically a part of Guadeloupe. They lie ten miles to the south of Basse-Terre and, with several good anchorages, are a popular separate attraction for the cruising yachtsman. The other offshore islands of Guadeloupe—La Désirade, Marie Galante, and Petite Terre—are only visited by adventurous types with lots of time on their hands.

The Saints are a popular vacation spot for Guadeloupe residents (many of whom have cottages there for use on weekends and holidays) and are also the target of local cruise boats from the Point-à-Pitre area, so the anchorages and shore facilities can be very crowded. The islands were settled by Breton fishermen (whose descendants can still be seen), but the quaint charm The Saints exhibited in the early Sixties when I first saw them has been submerged in the rising tide of tourism.

Speaking of local French boats, a word of warning on their anchoring practices is in order. This isn't a personal prejudice of mine; it is shared by all who operate wherever French boats do, and has been written about even in French publications. A great many French sailors are careless and thoughtless, anchoring too close or right over another boat's rode with little or no regard for how their own anchor is set. The result is frequent dragging and 0300 panic parties when these boats come bumping into you. Recently, this happened to me in the attractive Sugar Loaf anchorage in The Saints. A boat anchored right across our rode, but did move after a while, breaking out our anchor in the process and setting us adrift. Fortunately, this was on a relatively calm midafternoon.

Sugar Loaf is well protected off a pleasant beach. The other major anchorage is right off the town of Bourg des Saintes, which tends to be very crowded and busy with passing ferryboats and local launches.

Despite these drawbacks, The Saints are a pleasant break in the long haul between DesHayes and Dominica, the next island south.

Dominica

Mountainous, primitive Dominica, the poorest island in the Lesser Antilles economically, is also one of the most scenic, with high, jagged peaks, steep cliffs, and lush vegetation. Aside from its economic troubles (which were deepened by the devastation of Hurricane David in 1979), it has fewer harbors than any other Caribbean island. The best one is at Portsmouth at the north end, eighteen miles from The Saints. With two knobby promontories standing guard on each side of its wide entrance, and awesome Mount Diablotin, almost five thousand feet high, towering up to the south, Prince Rupert Bay is scenic and roomy. It's often subject to surge, and always subject to the forays of the "rowboat mafia," young boys who swarm around in incredibly crude rowboats at the entrance to the bay.

While the boys can be a nuisance, especially when you're trying to pick a spot to anchor, they can be helpful, too. Once you select one of the group as "your boy," he'll usually fend off the others and help by getting ice and fresh fruit and vegetables on shore. (Other than these, there are very few supplies available here.) The boys may also want to take you up the nearby Indian

River, a worthwhile excursion into a tropical jungle if you have the time to spare.

There's nothing but mountain scenery and a couple of small coves down the west coast of Dominica until Roseau, the capital, at the southwest end. This is an open, commercial roadstead, very deep and rolly, and no place for yachts to anchor. It's better to go a couple of miles south and tie stern-to at the Anchorage Hotel, but this too is a hotbed of rowboat gangs and a difficult place to lie. Roseau, like Portsmouth, is a port of entry.

At the south end of Dominica it's possible to find an uneasy anchorage at Soufrière or Scotts Head. But the best place to lie, if you have to stay over in this area, is Woodbridge Bay, just north of Roseau. Its shoreline is commercial, and the nearby river is the town sewer, but there's less likelihood of surge here, and the rowboat gangs aren't in evidence.

The most interesting thing to do on Dominica is to take a taxi ride up into the rain forests, which are unbelievably lush. As the dense green foliage closes in, brightly colored birds flit through trees and vines, and flowers add splotches of color.

Martinique

Most sophisticated of the Lesser Antilles is the big, mountainous island of Martinique, another department of France. At its north end, about twenty miles from Scotts Head at the south end of Dominica, infamous Mt. Pelee broods over the scene in an almost perpetual cover of clouds. St. Pierre, right under it, whose forty thousand inhabitants were wiped out by Pelee's eruption in 1902, is an open roadstead and not a good anchorage, though a visit to the volcano museum is worth a stop.

It's another twenty-five miles to Fort de France, Martinique's major city. A city it is, with about eighty thousand inhabitants and all sorts of shops, restaurants, markets, and hotels. Fort de France is a busy commercial harbor and a popular cruise-ship stop. Yachts have their own anchorage in Baie de Flammands, right off the Savanna, the center of Fort de France. A customs and immigration office is at the water's edge, making port formalities easy. With lots of passing sea traffic, Fort de France is a rolly place during the day, and the surge can be persistent. The harbor itself is also crowded, and the French anchoring tactics mentioned before are very much in evidence.

The bay of Fort de France is wide, and the trades can kick up a good chop in it. Around the bay's perimeter there are several more anchorages for yachts. The most popular is directly across from Baie de Flammands, at Anse Mitan, where there's a fine beach, and marinas, restaurants, hotels, boutiques, and facilities for water sports. Cohe de Lametin and Trois Ilets (birthplace of Napoleon's Josephine) are used by yachts.

South of Fort de France there's a pleasant anchorage, much favored by local boats for overnighting and weekending, called Anse d'Arlet. The center is buoyed off so that yachts don't interfere with local commercial fishermen, but there's good room along the sides of the bay, and good protection.

Someone with a great deal of time and a good ability for eyeball navigation may want to explore the less-visited parts of Martinique, like the St. Anne area at the southeast tip and the many bays and coves behind the fringing reef on the east coast. This is not a project to be undertaken lightly, as the passes through the reef are unmarked and must be negotiated in good light with the sun high, coming right in from the open, trade wind–swept Atlantic. Summer is the best time to pursue this sort of adventure.

St. Lucia

This island has several good harbors and has recently developed into an important charter base. Although it has these good cruising harbors, its comparative isolation makes for fairly long passages to harbors on the neighboring islands of Martinique and St. Vincent. For example, it's over twenty miles from the south end of Martinique to the first port on St. Lucia, Pigeon Island and Rodney Bay.

On the way south from Martinique is Diamond Rock, a prominent, five-hundred-foot pinnacle of rugged rock a mile off the south coast. It has an unusual place in history. In the late eighteenth century, the British managed to land a force on its almost vertical sides, complete with supplies and cannon, and make their way to the top using block and tackle. There they set up a base and hoisted the Union Jack, dubbing the pinnacle H.M.S. *Diamond Rock*. They kept a close watch on the movements of the French fleet in Martinique and signaled messages back by sun mirror to Admiral Rodney, sitting atop the fortified hill at Pigeon Island off St. Lucia. This tactic eventually enabled Rodney to meet and defeat the French fleet in a sea battle.

Pigeon Island is no longer an island, as it has been connected to the main island by a dredge-filled causeway. At the inner end is Rodney Bay, a port of entry, opened by dredging and now a secure charter base and marina.

St. Lucia, a long island, has several harbors on its west coast. It also has two airports—a jetport at Hewanorra at the very southern tip (a long taxi ride from the rest of the island), and a strip for interisland traffic at Vigie on Castries Harbor on the northwest coast. Castries is a commercial port with a good harbor but not much charm, as it was twice devastated by fire in the Forties and the modern buildings that have replaced the burned-out ones have a utilitarian look. Yachts use Vigie Cove on the north side of the harbor, where there is a good dockside supermarket, and there's a new haulout facility and fuel dock right off the end of the airstrip.

The major attraction on St. Lucia is Marigot Bay, which has recently been developed into a bareboat center and charter base. With perfect protection, especially in the inner harbor, which is almost completely enclosed by a palm-covered point extending from the north shore, Marigot Bay is a gracefully picturesque anchorage, set about with high hills. There are a hotel and restaurant on each side of the bay, connected by a continuously operated ferry launch. In the bay there is plenty of anchoring room; a small marina dock, called Hurricane Hole, lies on the south side. Some supplies are available in the limited commissary, but Marigot is otherwise a very complete service base and attractive cruising stop.

South of Marigot, the town of Soufrière offers stern-to mooring to trees, for eating ashore. The "rowboat mafia" is particularly active here, as it is at the spectacular Pitons a mile south. These twin cones are St. Lucia's trademark, and there's an anchorage at the beach between them, unusual in that anchors are set in deep water and stern lines are tied to trees ashore. This is one of the most scenic mooring spots anywhere in the islands (in 1985 it had the added attraction of a tame elephant "moored" to the beach, a startling sight to newcomers). It's worth the effort here to take the rugged climb to a waterfall a few hundred yards back of the beach.

Vieux Fort, near Hewanorra airport, is a possible anchorage right at the tip of the island, but it's usually a windward thrash to get there and probably not worth the trouble.

St. Vincent

St. Vincent is largely agricultural, and its mountainous slopes, leading up to the three-thousand-foot volcano Soufrière (which erupted on Friday the thirteenth of April, 1979), are extensively cultivated. The only two harbors to break the long run down the leeward side are Cumberland and Wallilabou Bays, where the usual line-to-a-tree mooring is necessary. Over the years, the natives here have been most unpleasantly insistent in soliciting incoming boats, to the point of abuse, and it might be smart to inquire about the current climate before stopping in.

Kingstown, the capital, on the south coast, is a rough, open commercial port and not recommended for yachts. Though Kingstown is a port of entry, the procedure is best done by taxi from the yacht anchorages at Blue Lagoon or Young Island. Food shopping must also be done in Kingstown by taxi, and it's interesting to combine a taxi ride with a visit to the Botanical Gardens. Young Island is protected and has a small, attractive luxury resort, but the current in the anchorage is strong and difficult to handle when anchoring. Blue Lagoon, base for a big bareboat fleet, is generally well-protected, though there's a low, persistent surge much of the time.

The Grenadines

The Grenadines are a string of small islands that stretch for sixty miles from St. Vincent to Grenada. They are split politically: St. Vincent owns Bequia, Union, Cannouan, and Mustique, and Grenada owns Carriacou and Petit Martinique at the southern end. But they're all of a piece as cruising grounds. Because of the difficulty of entering and clearing at Kingstown on St. Vincent, many skippers bypass the big island and enter at Bequia, where entry is a simple process right on the waterfront. Clifton, at Union Island, is the other port of entry for the St. Vincent Grenadines, and Carriacou serves as one for the Grenadian part. It's a nuisance to go through these formalities for islands that are so close and all part of the same cruising area, but the rubber-stamp bangers must be satisfied.

Bequia (pronounced "*bek*-wee"), five miles from Blue Lagoon, is almost always the first stop for the bareboats leaving there. Even if it weren't this close and weren't a port of entry it would be popular, because it's a picturesque island with a flavor of its own. Bequia has been a center for commercial sail through the years, though that has almost died out. Many fine island schooners were built there. The island also has a whaling industry of sorts, though this is now done more for show than for business, in graceful whaleboats like those used in the days of the "Nantucket Sleighride." A good year will see one or two whales brought to the dressing station.

Bequia's main harbor, Admiralty Bay at Port Elizabeth, is always filled with boats, and a good anchoring spot is hard to find, as space is limited in the shallow areas along the beach. The rest of the harbor is quite deep, and there's a reef just south of the main anchorage that sometimes catches the unaware. There's another anchorage a bit away from the town at Princess Margaret Beach, a half mile south, and Friendship Bay on the east side is pleasant but inclined to be surgy.

With good sailing breezes, gorgeous water colors, white-sand beaches on almost every island, great reefs for snorkeling and diving, interesting places to visit ashore, and a wide choice of harbors, these islands make an idyllic cruising ground. Sometimes wind blows more than anyone needs, as the trades are completely unblocked sweeping into the Grenadines, and there are interisland passages where seas sweep in unimpeded and build up well, particularly near the little rock known as Petit Cannouan. There are protected stretches, too.

Besides Bequia, popular stops include Mustique, a jet-set hideaway with a rolly anchorage, and Cannouan, Mayero, Palm Island, Union Island, Petit St. Vincent, Carriacou, and the number-one highlight, the Tobago Cays. These reef-girt, uninhabited islets in the middle of the chain are a national park, and only a few fishermen camp on the beaches. The snorkeling is tops, the beaches are beautiful, and the anchorage is secure and well protected unless the wind really gets boisterous.

Grenada

Following a ten-year ordeal of political upheaval, climaxing in October 1983 with the U.S. Intervention (which is what Grenadians prefer to call it, rather than "invasion"), Grenada is facing the future with hope, optimism, and a package full of problems. From a yachting point of view, Grenada is still about as attractive as any island in the Caribbean, and the events of 1983 should mean increased opportunities for enjoying its attractions.

The mammoth airstrip built by the Cubans at Point

Saline at the southern end of the island is now in operation, making Grenada much more accessible by air than when its only airport was the tiny Pearls strip, seventeen miles up the east coast. Moreover, Grenada's customs and immigration procedures have been streamlined to attract visitors by both air and sea.

Nautically, pending new developments by investors attracted by the cooperative post-Intervention atmosphere, there are two good yachting centers on Grenada. The Lagoon, an arm of the commercial harbor at St. George's, was opened to yachts after a dredging project in the Sixties that cleared a channel through the bar to deep water. Subsequently, Grenada Yacht Services marina and yard were built, a first-rate facility that was the yachting capital of the lower Caribbean until the political upheavals drove visitors away.

Yachts started coming back soon after the Intervention, and GYS, despite its inevitably run-down condition, is busy again. The Lagoon provides a good anchorage area and is an easy dinghy ride to the town's well-stocked supermarkets, native fresh-food market, and other shops. There's a constant parade of people through GYS looking for work or selling wares, and cheap labor is therefore plentiful. (Before help is taken on, however, a reference on the worker should be obtained.)

The south coast is scenically very pleasant and is a delightful area for gunkholing. Good cruising harbors include L'Anse aux Epines (called "Lansapeen" or Prickly Bay), Hartman's Bay, Clark's Court Bay, Hog Island, and Port Egmont. There are a boatyard and a charter center at L'Anse aux Epines.

Although Glenville, on the east coast, is a port, it's not well set up for yachts. The only other anchorage on

Grenada is Halifax Harbor on the west coast, a few miles north of St. George's. Drawbacks here are a newly established garbage dump on shore and the operations of fishermen, who work their nets very early in the morning.

Halifax's main advantage is that it gives a bit of a head start to a boat making the long passage back up the chain of islands to Carriacou. Still, it's often a rough trip, due to heavy chop in the area of "Kick 'em Jenny" (on the chart as Diamond Rock) and a strong westbound current. It's usually wise to hug the coast of Grenada, motorsailing if necessary, all the way around the northern tip to the bay off Sauteurs before squaring away for Carriacou. It's always a relief to get into well-protected Tyrell Bay there, as the reverse trip northward up the islands should be a reach from then on.

Bay Islands of Honduras

Although we're mainly concerned with the eastern Caribbean, there are two cruising areas in the western Caribbean that are available to visitors. The Bay Islands off the coast of Honduras—Roatan, Utila, Guanaja, and the Cochinos being the main attractions—are a bareboat area. The atmosphere is much more primitive than in the bustling eastern Caribbean, and there are many good harbors close together, among them the charter base at Brick Harbor on the south coast of Roatan and a major diving center at Anthony's Cay on the north coast. Coxen Hole, French Harbor, Caribe Point Bight, Port Royal, and Oak Ridge Harbor are also good spots on the south coast of Roatan. The Cochinos are particularly pleasant. The islanders here speak English (the islands were British until the mid-nineteenth century), and the climate is like that in the eastern Caribbean, except that winter northers are experienced more often.

Belize

The barrier reef off the Central American country of Belize (formerly British Honduras) is the second largest in the world (Australia's Great Barrier Reef is largest) and makes for wonderful, away-from-it-all cruising, with bareboats available. There are very few other boats there, and the wonders of the reef as well as jungle rivers on the mainland, like the Sitee, can be explored in solitude. Lighthouse Reef, Turneffe Reef, Glover's Reef, and Tobacco Cay are some of the more attractive anchorages.

VI

Support Systems

Depending on what kind of boat you're on, there are varying degrees of worry about services and provisioning, the day-to-day nitty-gritty of operating a boat in these islands. Of course, if you're on a professionally crewed charter, you need only sit back and relax, because all problems are taken care of by the captain and crew. Your only worries might be where to shop for the best bargains, a subject discussed later in this chapter. A fleet bareboat should be well provisioned if you order it that way, but if you opt for partial provisioning you may end up doing some extra food shopping, and this can be an adventure. And, naturally, if you're on a private boat or an individually arranged bareboat charter, all provisioning is up to you.

A similar situation applies to service. Bareboats seldom get so far away from home base that a chase boat cannot reach them if there are mechanical difficulties, although it's good to know where service yards and mechanics are in case of emergency. Again, the individually operated boat is on its own.

Services

There are very few harbors in the eastern Caribbean where it's impossible to locate a mechanic. Unemployment is high, so enterprising types put their mechanical skills to good use. I've dealt with mechanics on almost every island at one time or another, and I've found it surprising how competent they are with little formal training. Our boatkeeper's mechanic in Tortola, for example, who comes from St. Vincent, said he learned about diesel engines by messing around with tractors on the farm where he grew up. Most mechanics shrug and say, "Oh, I just picked it up," when asked how they learned their trade. Once or twice, a complete phony has talked his way on board, only to be discovered and dismissed.

There are also men from all over the world who have ended up in the Caribbean as crew on a passage yacht, and have decided to stay and make a living from their mechanical or electrical skills. We've seen Americans, Canadians, South Africans, Dutchmen, Englishmen, Aussies, and many more scratching out this kind of existence. Some connect up with marinas or diesel repair shops, while others free-lance.

Some areas are almost devoid of service yards, but, as the tide of yachting involvement has swelled all through the islands, more and more marinas and service yards have opened. About the only place we've had trouble finding a mechanic was in Dominica. But there could be outlying harbors in the Grenadines and some small ports on the big islands like Guadeloupe and St. Vincent where it would be equally hard to locate one. In general, anywhere there's a charter service there's sure to be mechanics and other types of experts. All the major ports, for example, have service yards. Then, too, there are several in the Fajardo area of Puerto Rico, as well as in St. Thomas. The B.V.I. have service centers at West End, Nanny Cay, Road Town, Maya Cove, and Virgin Gorda Yacht Harbour.

St. Martin has two service yards on Great Bay—Philipsburg, and one inside Simson Lagoon. We found an auto mechanic in St. Barts to work on a water pump impeller. Antigua has yards at St. John's, English Harbour, and Parham Sound, and Guadeloupe's Point-à-Pitre area is a likely spot to find service there. As mentioned, Dominica was a hard place for us to get serviced, but there are mechanics to be found there. Fort de France, a major city, has all services. Blue Lagoon on St. Vincent has mechanics, as do Bequia, Clifton, and Carriacou in the Grenadines. The Lagoon and L'Anse aux Epines at Grenada have good services.

There aren't as many haulout yards as mechanics to be found, as such facilities are fairly well spread out. Of the aforementioned harbors, Fajardo and Isleta Marina in Puerto Rico have lifts, as does Charlotte Amalie, The Lagoon, and Red Hook on St. Thomas. West End, Nanny Cay, Road Town, and Virgin Gorda Yacht Harbour are haulout spots in the B.V.I., as are Bobby's Marina and Simson Lagoon in St. Martin (there's a primitive railway on the French side at Marigot). Antigua has facilities at the Slipway and Crabbs, and Guadeloupe at Point-à-Pitre. Martinique has several, including a commercial yard for ships. There are haulout facilities on St. Lucia (in Rodney Bay and Castries), on St. Vincent and Bequia, and, farther south in the Grenadines, at Clifton and Union islands. Grenada Yacht Services at The Lagoon can handle large yachts.

Almost every yard that does haulouts also has a chandlery where routine equipment can be bought, but major replacements like water pumps and engine blocks must come from the States and take a long time to be delivered. If you do need spare parts sent, St. Martin is a good place to receive them, as it's a duty-free island without any customs. As a matter of practice, I keep as many spare engine parts on board as possible, and have replacements sent from the States as soon as they're used.

There are sailmakers and sail repair shops in Puerto Rico, St. Thomas, Tortola, St. Martin (where I had a furniture upholsterer repair a staysail nicely and inexpensively), Antigua, the French islands, St. Lucia, St. Vincent, and the Grenadines. A sailmaking kit on board is a good idea if there's someone skillful enough to use it.

There are inflatable-boat dealers who can repair dinghies (or sell you a new one) in most of the major centers, and outboard motors can be serviced almost everywhere.

Provisioning

This section is for individually operated boats, or for bareboats that have only been partially stocked by the fleet operator. In some parts of the Caribbean, provisioning is as easy as at the neighborhood supermarket at home, while in other areas it's quite an adventure. In general, prices are shockingly high by Stateside standards, because everything except a few native fruits, vegetables, and fish must be imported.

In many areas, the native produce is sold at sidewalk stands by elderly women, and it's possible to shop around and do quite well on quality. Prices at these stands are also a bit lower than in the stores. (The supermarket in Road Town, Tortola, for example, once had imported limes for seventy-five cents apiece, while a native woman down the street was selling the smaller but juicier local variety for fifty cents a half dozen.) The best buys in native produce are in bananas, limes, tomatoes, cucumbers, lettuce, celery, eggplant, carrots, cristofine, and tanya. Tanya is similar to a yam. Cristofine is a lumpy, squashlike food that must be peeled with hands greased by butter, oleo, or Pam, as its skin has tiny spikes. It tastes best when cooked with ginger root. Many of the islands have their own special delights. For instance, I'll take the dinghy a long way to get fresh, hot croissants for breakfast.

Native fish and lobster are usually fine, but almost all other meat except goat is imported (mostly from New Zealand) and frozen. As elsewhere, chicken is usually one of the better bargains. In the French islands, everything is imported from France, so the packaged goods are of the French variety. Most of the other islands have the familiar American brand names in canned goods and other dry stores.

In all the big towns there are large, well-stocked markets. Often, they're a taxi ride away, but at some spots they're located right on the waterfront or in the marina. This is true at Nanny Cay, Road Town, Virgin Gorda Yacht Harbour, Philipsburg, Marigot, St. Barts, St. John, English Harbour, Fort de France (though the best one here is inland), Vigie, Clifton, Bequia, Carriacou, and St. George's. In the smaller towns like Bequia and Hillsborough, one takes potluck on what's available and must shop around in several small spots before finding adequate supplies. (We always take large canvas tote bags with us to market to make carrying easier.)

While food is expensive, liquor is relatively cheap, as it is all or partly duty-free in most places. A bottle of Mount Gay rum that is over ten dollars in the States will be anywhere from three to four and a half dollars in the islands, and cheaper by the case in some places. It's surprising to compare liquor prices and find that stores within a few yards of each other have quite different prices. Rum, of course, is a bargain, though local brands are distilled differently on various islands, and the quality can vary. A strong, sugary aroma wafts up from these relatively unrefined rums.

Beer and wine don't offer the bargains that hard liquor does in the Caribbean, probably because of transporting costs. In the out-of-the-way places, one sometimes has to make do with rather strange choices in wine, but the well-known European and American brands are available in the larger stores. European and American beers are sold at about the same price here.

Currencies

The currency matter is not a problem in the Caribbean, as American money is almost universally accepted—paper money, that is. Except where it's the official currency, as in the B.V.I., American coins aren't welcome, and they aren't good to tip with.

The guilder is the official monetary unit in the Dutch islands, but the American visitor hardly ever sees a guilder, as the dollar is everywhere accepted. In the French islands, the franc is the official monetary unit, and the French, characteristically, are not as willing to take dollars (although the recent strength of the dollar has changed this somewhat). You almost always get change in francs after paying in dollars.

Barbados has its own currency, useful information if you happen to stop there on a plane connection, but the rest of the former British islands use Eastern Caribbean currency, or E.C. The exchange rate was 2.60 U.S. dollars to the E.C. dollar in 1985. For me, it's always a shock to be quoted a price that seems very high, only to realize it's in E.C. currency. When U.S. dollars are presented, E.C. change is almost always given, so there can be great confusion in trying to use both U.S. and E.C. in settling transactions. Somehow I always seem to get stuck with some E.C. currency when it's time to go home.

That other universal currency—plastic money, otherwise known as credit cards—is widely accepted in shops and restaurants in the Caribbean, but not everywhere by any means, and certainly not in food stores.

I find it a handy practice to take a packet of fifty one-dollar bills with me on each trip to the Caribbean. It makes tipping easy, and settling small accounts and purchases is a lot simpler with ones, because getting change for larger bills can sometimes be avoided.

Shopping

Some people seem to travel just to shop, even on sailboat cruises in the Caribbean. And there are plenty of opportunities for every kind of shopping, for anything from souvenir T-shirts to expensive jewelry and perfumes, at least in the larger cities and towns. St. Thomas is perhaps the busiest cruise-ship port in the world, largely because it provides duty-free shopping for luxury items and liquor. When several cruise ships are in port, the narrow main street of Charlotte Amalie is jammed with eager shoppers looking for bargains in perfume, jewelry, cameras, binoculars, clothes, and even furs, as well as the little gimcracks to take home as gifts or keep as souvenirs. The *bang-bang* of credit card machines is the dominant sound. And when sailing time comes, the street is suddenly strangely silent again—until the next invasion of tourists.

Philipsburg and Marigot on St. Martin, and the French shops in St. Barts, Guadeloupe, and Martinique are all busy with sales of luxury items. Fort de France, the biggest city in the Lesser Antilles, is especially well set up for this.

In addition to the obvious bargains in luxury items, some of the islands have native handwork that is well worth considering. Batik blouses and skirts are popular in the B.V.I. and in many of the lower islands, as are items like small woven baskets and hats. T-shirts for sale are ubiquitous, with every kind of logo, from understated alligators to blaring psychedelic scenes, and with messages sentimental, humorous, and pornographic. Usually, they don't fit very well, and they wear out quickly.

Some broad advice on shopping is to shop carefully, making sure you really want an item and have room to keep it on board and to pack it when you go home. Avoid shopping in towns like Charlotte Amalie, Philipsburg, and Fort de France on days when cruise ships are in port. The elbowing competition at the counters is pretty rough, and salespeople as a result are harried and unable to give you the kind of service you might want.

VII

Eating Ashore

In addition to the challenge of the shopping quest, eating ashore is another Caribbean adventure. Even on crewed charters, where meals are paid for in advance, many cruisers like to break up the routine and sample life on shore occasionally. Not only is it a change of scene and a chance to explore, it gives the professional cook on board a small respite from the constant demands of that job. Unless your budget is very tight, it's a good idea, for the same reasons, to plan for a few meals ashore on a bareboat cruise, too.

When we first cruised the British Virgin Islands in 1964, there was only one place where people from a visiting yacht could eat ashore—Marina Cay. Today, one could eat ashore every night for a month and still not sample every restaurant. There's a wide choice of places to go, not only in the B.V.I., but all through the islands.

There is also a wide choice of cuisines: West Indian, Creole, Indonesian, Chinese, French, Italian, and American, to name a few. For those who like to try local cuisine while traveling, be aware that West Indian cooking leans heavily on spices and sauces, mainly in seafood and chicken dishes. Rice is used a lot, and local staples include plantain (a bananalike fruit that must be cooked to be eaten), cristofine (a squashlike vegetable, as earlier explained), tanya (a potato substitute), cucumbers, and carrots. Popular fishes include dolphin (the fish, not the mammal, of course), snapper, grouper, kingfish, old wife, wahoo, and swordfish. Conch, rubbery and tough to start with, when properly tenderized through laborious beating is great eating in a highly spiced peppery salad or stew. Or else, try it fried or in fritters.

The Caribbean lobster, or langouste, is a crayfish, clawless in contrast to the familiar cold-water variety. It's perhaps not as tender as northern lobster, but is sweet and tasty, and is served in a number of ways: broiled, baked, Newburg, and in other types of cream sauce. Even though this lobster is local, it's not inexpensive, because overfishing has reduced the supply. It's protected from spearfishermen in most areas, and is only available abundantly in areas of extensive reefs, like Anegada in the northern B.V.I., Anguilla, Barbuda, and the Grenadines, where commercial lobstermen operate.

Again, a word of warning about eating fish you catch yourself, especially in the northern Caribbean. Ciguatera is a problem. This unpleasant form of poisoning often causes nausea, fever, and weakness, and also a strange effect in which cold and heat on the flesh produce reverse sensations. Rain falling against a ciguatera victim's skin feels like fire. In restaurants and markets, however, the fish can be presumed safe, as the local fishermen know where the fish come from and how to avoid contaminated ones.

As mentioned, there's very little local meat except goat (and I must confess I haven't tried it). In the markets and restaurants, the steaks, chops, and veal are all imported. Depending on the island, this can be from North America, New Zealand, or Europe, making the meat expensive, but the quality of meat is generally high at the better restaurants. At native-run restaurants, beef and chops can be of poor quality and tough, so it's usu-

Eating Ashore

ally smarter to stick to local cooking of fish or chicken in these places.

Native fruits and vegetables are generally delicious. Limes, grapefruits, and oranges are grown locally on most islands, and the local bananas can be excellent in season (especially the little sugar bananas, hardly bigger than fat fingers). Sugar apples, very sweet and sticky, mangos, and pawpaws are local fruits that may be on dessert menus, but there are very few places where local pineapple is available. Breads and pastries are very good eating, especially on the French islands. And be very explicit when ordering martinis, or you'll get vermouth on the rocks.

Almost all places require reservations. Sometimes it's enough to take the dinghy ashore on arrival and make arrangements then, but most restaurants that cater to cruising sailors man VHF radios (usually Channel 16 for calling, and then a switch to another frequency), and they like to be given as much advance notice as possible, even as regards menu selections. Credit cards are generally, but not universally, accepted, and it's always a good idea to inquire ahead of time. The practice of applying the tip directly to the bill as a service charge is widely used, but again not universally, and an inquiry should be made about this matter when settling.

Dress is almost universally casual. Some places prefer that men be in long pants, but I only know of two out of the eighty or so spots we've been to over the years where a coat and tie are needed. Curtain Bluff, a hotel on Antigua, requires coat and tie for all but one beach buffet night, and the rule is suspended during Antigua Race Week. Peter Island Yacht Club in the B.V.I. has certain nights when coats and ties are a requirement in the dining room. It's best to make sure about any dress code when making a reservation.

In ambience, Caribbean restaurants run the gamut from plain board tables and home-style serving to the most sophisticated crystal, silver, and white tablecloths in a city establishment. Many restaurants are on the water, with attractive views across an anchorage; some are in the hills, with panoramic views. In the interest of economy, we usually choose a restaurant within walking distance of an anchorage, but sometimes a taxi ride has to be added. (Often, restaurants will have a special taxi working for them at established rates, and arrangements can be made for a ride while making reservations.)

The style of serving varies. Some places have a fixed, full-course menu, while others serve à la carte. A buffet is the answer in places that keep an informal atmosphere and have fewer employees. Several women who have cruised with us prefer à la carte service or a buffet, since they are light eaters and hate to have a great hearty meal thrust in front of them. They are happy with appetizer, soup, and dessert, for example, or soup and salad.

Personal recommendations on restaurants are tricky, as tastes vary, and restaurants come and go. They either disappear, or management changes, and the place I knew could be completely different. Also, although there are seventy-five establishments listed below, there are many places I haven't been that could be as good or better than those I mention. Because a place isn't listed means nothing against it. It just means I haven't been there. This applies especially to big cities, such as San Juan, Charlotte Amalie, and Fort de France, where there are dozens of good places. In the western Caribbean I've only eaten ashore once, at Anthony's Cay on Roatan, an active diving center.

Eating Ashore

There are a few places on the list that I haven't been to myself, but they've been recommended by crew members or friends. Also, this personal list of places visited between 1980 and 1985 is heavy on the B.V.I. because we've spent more time there than in other areas, there are more eating places there per square mile, and, since the distances port-to-port are small, it's easier to get in and make arrangements here than at the end of a fifty-mile interisland thrash farther down the Lesser Antilles.

Taking nothing away from the places that are merely listed, there are some spots that deserve special mention because we've especially enjoyed them or because they have some special feature that sets them apart.

In going through my logbooks to research this list, I found that we've been to The Last Resort in Trellis Bay in the B.V.I. forty-six times since starting to operate there. That's a lot of visits, especially since the "floor show," amusing songs and patter by Tony Snell, who runs the place with his wife Jacquie, has always been the same. The reason for our patronage is that the buffet dinner is always excellent, the best food for the money in the area, and the show, no matter how often you hear it, is very funny. This is a "one-off" place, with nothing else like it the Caribbean, or anywhere else, for that matter. The show is a bit ribald, perhaps not suited to your Aunt Nellie, but our grandchildren, who didn't understand some of the innuendos, thought it was great. An added attraction is a pet donkey, Chocolate, who puts her head through a specially framed opening into the bar to check on things several times during an evening.

Almost equally popular with us is Bitter End Yacht Club on Gorda Sound, a well-run, nautically oriented resort that welcomes yachtsmen (by the hundreds, sometimes) for dinner, and handles them with awesome efficiency, serving fine food. My records show we've been there twenty-six times.

Two mountaintop restaurants on Tortola deserve special mention. The Cloud Room, run by a Tortolan family, is set so high on a mountain overlooking Road Town, with a fantastic view over Drake Channel to the southwest, that a special free bus, run by the proprietor, Paul Watley, is needed to get people there. Paul picks people up at various Road Town locations and returns them afterward. Aside from the thrill of the ride and the great view, the food is very good.

Equally high, and with a wider all-around view, is Sky World, near the western end of Tortola. We've only been there for lunch, but this is the best time to go to enjoy the view. Brandywine Bay is not so high up, though it's atop a point just east of Road Town and has a commanding view, with food as good as can be found in the area. Olde Yard Inn on Virgin Gorda, with pleasant food and atmosphere, has an unusual library carefully arranged in glass cases, a former private collection that is surprising to find in this part of the world.

On Anguilla, a beachfront spot called The Barrel Stay, at Sandy Ground, has as much local atmosphere as you can find and good local food, such as conch. In contrast, La Grenouille, in Philipsburg, St. Martin, is very civilized and sophisticated, with a fine continental menu. It's beachfront, too, though one flight up. Other Dutch-side restaurants that have proved good are Chesterfield's, Antoine's, and Pinochio's, and the French side has a host of good restaurants along the quay in Marigot and in Grand Case. Some we've enjoyed are La Vie en Rose, Boucanier, La Calanque, and Le Nadillac in Marigot. La Nacelle and the Fish Pot in Grand Case are supposed to be good, but I haven't sampled them.

Eating Ashore

St. Barts is loaded with eating places, but we haven't had much chance to try them. Two that we sampled a few years ago are closed, and at La Cremaillere the food was good but the service was terrible. Le Chastenets is supposed to be the best spot on St. Barts, but I've never gotten ashore soon enough to get a reservation.

The Admiral's Inn at English Harbour, Antigua, reeks with atmosphere and is the gathering place for yachtsmen. Another fascinating spot is the restaurant on top of Shirley Heights, overlooking English Harbour from a magnificent vantage point. The native-run Catamaran Club on Falmouth Harbour does a very nice job, with a terrace right at the water's edge. The best place I've found on Antigua is the aforementioned Curtain Bluff. Its harbor is sometimes a bit surgy, but it's possible to get out of the surge at nearby Carlisle Bay and dinghy over, as long as you have a coat and tie. If you do, it's worth it.

We haven't eaten ashore on Guadeloupe, but I've been told that the unpretentious-looking café at the town pier in DesHayes has excellent native food at a good price, despite the surroundings.

One could make a career of eating out in Martinique at Fort de France and Anse Mitan alone. There are European-standard restaurants, and there's a wide choice. Right on the harbor at Baie de Flammands, Fort de France, with its own dinghy dock, is La Grand Voile. If you go, spring for the "gastronomic" menu rather than the standard one. There's a difference in price, but it's worth it. There are perhaps a dozen good restaurants on the peninsula near the Hotel Bakoua at Anse Mitan, across the bay from Fort de France.

At Marigot Bay, St. Lucia, the Doolittle Restaurant on the north side of the harbor is particularly pleasant, and The Hummingbird at Soufrière, where you tie stern-to-tree, is interesting and good for local food.

Now that Grenada has made a tourist-business comeback, the restaurants there have perked up. We had an excellent dinner at one called Cinnamon Hill, and a native place called Mamma's, just up the hill from Grenada Yacht Services, puts out the most amazing array of native foods at a price of twenty-five dollars E.C. (about ten dollars U.S.). Platters keep coming (along with brief speeches of identification)—coucou, callalou, breadfruit, octopus, plantain, cristofine, snapper, and lobster, among many others. If you want the genuine article in dining out in the Caribbean, this is it.

Listed alphabetically by island are restaurants of which I have personal knowledge.

> Anguilla: Barrel Stay
> Antigua: Admiral's Inn, Antigua Yacht Club, Catamaran, Curtain Bluff, Dockside (St. James's), Halcyon Cove, Shirley Heights
> Bay Islands: Anthony's Cay, Roatan
> British Virgins: Abe's (native), Bananas, Bath & Turtle (fast food), Biras Creek, Bitter End Yacht Club, Brandywine Bay, Carib Casseroles, CSY Marina, Cloud Room, Conch Shell Point (native), Cooper Island, Drake's Anchorage, Downstairs (fast food), Fisher's Cove, Fort Burt, Leverick Bay, Little Dix, Marina Cay, Mariner's Inn, Nanny Cay Snack Bar (fast food), Olde Yard Inn, Peace and Love (native), Peg Leg Landing, Peter Island Yacht Club, Prospect Reef, Rhymer's (native), Sky World, Stanley's (native), Sugar Mill, Treasure Isle, Upstairs, Virgin Queen, The Wharf
> Dominica: The Anchorage Hotel
> Grenada: Cinnamon Hill, Mamma's, The Nutmeg, Red Crab

Eating Ashore

Grenadines: Frangipanni (Bequia), The Spring (Bequia), Sunny Caribbee (Bequia), Palm Island, Petit St. Vincent, The Mermaid (Carriacou)
Guadeloupe: Native Cave, DesHayes
Martinique: Bakoua Hotel, Le Grande Voile, Les Flammands
St. Barts: Chastenets, La Cremaillere, Village St. Jean
St. Lucia: Coal Pot, Doolittle, Hummingbird, Hurricane Hole
St. Martin (Dutch side): Antoine's, Chesterfield, Le Galion, La Grenouille, Pinochio, Sam's, Summit Hotel
St. Martin (French side): Boucanier, La Calanque, Fish Pot, La Nacelle, Tropicana, La Vie en Rose
St. Vincent: CSY ((Blue Lagoon), Young Island

Prices don't vary as much as might be imagined. The price range for a dinner ashore runs between eighteen and twenty-six dollars for the meal, with drinks extra. Especially in the French restaurants, prices tend to be a bit higher, and wine prices would also be up there. Even the less fancy places tend to have prices that aren't far below the level of luxury spots.

VIII

Anchoring

In watching Caribbean operations over the years, and in being a part of them, I've become convinced that anchoring is the number-one problem in boat handling there. With bareboats the largest group numerically in most harbors, with Frenchmen increasingly in evidence, and with more and more private boats on hand, anchoring may now have become the single most important element in cruising seamanship in the area. Even the professional boats have their moments. Indeed, the letter column of a regional publication, *Caribbean Boating*, was steaming through the spring of 1985 with accusations back and forth between two charter-boat skippers over their anchoring techniques and behavior.

Most Caribbean harbors have become very crowded, which adds to the importance of proper anchoring. As an example, a boat we were near in Freeman Bay, outside English Harbour, Antigua, had been left untended on what must have been excessive scope. While the wind was strong from its normal easterly direction, she rode well and clear of the boats around her. During the night, however, the wind went fitful and the boat started to wander. She ended up nudging three boats in her travels. Perhaps there hadn't been boats that near when she was left, but Freeman Bay is a perpetually busy anchorage, and she'd been given too much scope for it.

With the thought that successful anchoring makes the

Anchoring

difference between a pleasant Caribbean cruise and a nerve-wracking one, the following observations are offered on the subject.

Some sailors approach anchoring with too much anxiety and timidity, while others have a cavalier attitude and pay insufficient attention. In either case, the results can be disastrous. There's no great mystery about anchoring once the requirements and techniques are understood. It's also a matter of equipment, and in the case of bareboats, the fleet operator should provide a main anchor that generally suits the range of nonextreme conditions the boat can be expected to meet. Spare anchors should take care of the special occasions of storms or the use of more than one anchor. There should be sufficient nylon rode for the expected operating area, with a shot of several fathoms of chain at the anchor end. In areas of prevalent coral, all-chain may be required. If all-chain is used, a "shock-absorber" pennant of nylon rode from the boat to the top of the chain is advisable.

Types of Anchors

Anchor types could be the subject of an entire book. The main ones in use are the CQR (plow), Danforth and Danforth-type, Bruce, Herreshoff, Northill, and the old-fashioned yachtsman's. The first two make up by far the greatest percentage of anchors in general use and usually fill the bill. Weight depends on the size of the boat and the type of anchor. Danforths can be quite light if given enough scope, and once they've taken hold they have tremendous holding power. Their weakness shows when the boat swings quickly to a new heading in a strong wind shift or gust; this can break the anchor out, and it may have trouble resetting. A beer can on the fluke or a clam shell between them can also foul the Danforth, making it ineffective.

The plow anchor, which is in use on more bareboats in the charter fleets than any other anchor, is very serviceable in most conditions. It has trouble penetrating weeds over hard sand, as do all anchors, and it sometimes has trouble in very soft, light sand, but it adapts well to most conditions. Also, since the stock isn't rigidly attached, but can move from side to side on a form of swivel, the plow swings around well when the boat takes a new heading, without pulling out. One thing to watch with a plow: if it hasn't set well it can drag very slowly, and a careful set of bearings should be kept, with frequent checks, to guard against this.

My heavily built CSY 37 cutter came equipped with a twenty-five-pound CQR, which had evidently proved itself in bareboat fleet operations, but I decided to move up to thirty-five pounds, and this has worked very well. When using a plow, roller-chock stowage at the stemhead is practically mandatory, as stowage is difficult otherwise. We do have our twenty-five-pound plow in a locker as a spare, and use a Danforth 13S to anchor fore and aft in harbors that call for that operation.

Selecting the Spot

No matter what the anchor, it must be handled properly to be effective. The best-designed anchor in the world can easily fail if it hasn't been set properly, and even then there's more to anchoring than just setting the hook. Selection of the spot in which to drop the anchor is of vital importance and involves a great many factors. First, you must know the depth of the water. Fortunately, in the Caribbean, this remains about con-

Anchoring

stant with the chart soundings, as there's very little rise and fall of tide.

Next, you should have some idea, if possible, of what type of bottom it is. Most charts include this information. In the Caribbean, eyeballing the color of the water, plus actual observation through its clear depths, can give a good idea of bottom type. In southern waters it's also important to have an idea of the colors that indicate coral heads, which obviously should be avoided. It takes some practice to tell the difference between dark patches that mean grass and dark patches that mean coral. Head for clear white sand if you possibly can.

Knowledge of bottom type can affect the amount of scope. In general, soft mud and soft sand require greater scope than firmer bottoms. Also, if you have a choice of anchor types, bottom type might affect the kind of anchor you use. In the Caribbean, it's usually easy to pick out a clear, sandy patch of bottom.

Once these general considerations are taken into account, the next step is to pick an exact spot in relation to the other boats already at anchor or moorings. In this respect, an empty mooring should be treated as though a boat were already in it, since one might come in later and pick it up. This is one of the common sins in anchoring courtesy: blocking someone else's mooring by anchoring too close, or actually fouling it. Also, never pick up a mooring without permission and without knowing its capacity. It might be for a dinghy.

The spot selected should allow you to swing in a 360° arc and clear all other boats that would be swinging the same way. In a harbor where the wind direction can be counted on to be steady, this isn't too great a problem. But where erratic backwinding and errant gusts from all directions are possible, especially in harbors under fairly high hills, plenty of room must be allowed. At Jost

Van Dyke I once had a boat come nudging alongside me at 0300 on a night of very light but vagrant breezes, and when I came on deck to see what was happening, its crew berated me for dragging. I checked my bearings and answered that we weren't dragging, and got the irate answer: "We can't be dragging. We have two hundred feet of scope out!" This is a harbor with about fifteen feet of depth. They weren't dragging. They were simply wandering all over the place on their long tether in every shift of the light air.

In other words, try to figure out all the swings you might make with the amount of scope you need (5:1 to 7:1 under most conditions), and anchor accordingly.

Anchoring Techniques

When approaching the selected spot, head into the wind (unless there's a current stronger than the wind, which would probably make it an undesirable spot to anchor at all). It's very salty to anchor under sail, but in a boat with auxiliary power, especially in a crowded harbor, it's very much the better part of valor to have the sails furled neatly and to maneuver under power. I must admit, I always leave the sail covers off and have the main halyard attached when maneuvering to anchor—just in case. If the sails are up and your boat veers off at enough of an angle to fill them while in the middle of the anchoring process, it can cause all sorts of complications. If anchoring under sail is necessary, at least get the foredeck clear by dousing the jib.

Just beyond the spot selected for the anchor to hit bottom, put the boat in reverse (or drop back with lost way if under sail) and ease the anchor over the bow under control. The Texas-cowboy approach to anchoring, also known as the shot-put technique, is not recom-

Anchoring

mended. Throwing the anchor over in a flying mass of line is sure to cause a fouling.

Let the engine or the wind take the boat back almost as far as the desired scope (mark the anchor line with tabs to tell you how much is out) and snub the line to see if the anchor has caught. If it has, the line will go taut and the boat will stop sliding sideways and swing into the wind. Watch the stern for this. If it feels as though the anchor has taken hold, let out scope to the desired distance and snub again, again checking the feel of the line and the swing of the stern. If everything seems OK, it's still a good idea to stay by the line for a few minutes, feeling its tension and watching the boat's swing. This is the time to take bearings on objects lined up ashore, or on fixed moorings, for future checking. If everything seems to be secure, then it's OK to start happy hour.

If you're in a situation where two anchors seem necessary—that is, if a blow is expected—the second anchor should be rowed out at an angle of about forty-five degrees to the other. This can be done without the dinghy by maneuvering the boat to both anchor drops, using extra scope to allow for the moves, then tightening up. I'm amazed at how many boats put out two anchors in a secure harbor on a night when no weather threatens. If the first anchor is set properly, the rest is wasted effort.

When forced to anchor in a tideway, the two-anchor Bahamian moor can be helpful. In this, anchors are set in a line perpendicular to the bow of the boat, one anchor leading off each bow. The boat ends up halfway between them, locked in position so that she'll swing first to one anchor and then to the other as the tide turns.

Straight fore-and-aft anchoring, sometimes advisable in very tight anchorages (the inner harbor at Gustavia,

St. Barts, is a prime example) or where there's a lot of backwinding and erratic swinging, is done by the same technique as the Bahamian moor, but the second anchor leads off the stern, rather than from the opposite bow chock. If you do anchor bow-and-stern, be sure that boats near you won't swing into you if they're on one anchor. Conversely, don't anchor close to a boat that is anchored bow-and-stern if you don't intend to do the same thing.

While the techniques of setting the anchor are of paramount importance, breaking out the anchor and getting under way require the right actions too. The secret here is to let the boat do the work. If you must sail off the hook, be sure to have the anchor rode straight up and down before letting the sail fill. If you haven't been able to break it out by hand, the boat may be able to do it as the sail fills. If under power, snub the rode when it comes short stay and let the forward momentum of the boat break it out.

In all anchoring and weighing procedures, I strongly recommend the use of hand signals between foredeck and cockpit. A lot of useless shouting and misunderstandings take place when they're not used. Hand signals can be very simple: just a wave forward for ahead and back for astern, a raised hand for stop, and a downward or upward motion of the hand for throttle changes. Mere pointing in the desired direction takes care of the boat's heading. A word of warning: it's easy to get interested in other boats in the anchorage and start pointing at them, causing all sorts of confusion at the helm.

All in all, though, anchoring is really very simple, isn't it? (Except when you do everything right and drag anyway. It happens to everyone.)

IX

Practical Matters

While anchoring may be the most important aspect of seamanship for pleasant Caribbean cruising, there are other seamanship factors and practical matters to consider. Although the weather is generally benign, the Caribbean can put boats and sailors to the test as can any body of open water.

Stowage

A simple thing like proper stowage before setting out is important, and sometimes disastrous if ignored. Before every sail, no matter how calm the weather or short the distance, we have a routine on our boat of checking through the cabins to make sure there's nothing loose lying around. Items on open shelves are tucked down, and shelves with sliding or hinged doors are securely closed. Galley equipment is stowed, hatches are closed, and ports are tightly dogged. We used to keep our dinghy oars on deck under the dinghy, but having lost one in rough weather, we now put them below.

On deck, loose items are secured or taken below. People do it, but I hate to see a boat sailing along with laundry strung along the lifelines. The sun and breeze are good for drying, but to me, port seems the better place for this chore. Laundry can blow away under sail, and can cause a tangle if there's a sudden sail drill. But my main objection is the poor esthetics.

If the anchor is in a bow chock, as it is on so many charter boats, it should be securely tied down, and the chain or rode on deck should be cleated with no play in it.

One simple and worthwhile practice in busy harbors is the tying off of halyards when at anchor or in a slip. There's nothing more annoying than the *whap-whap-whap* of halyards against aluminum, and it only takes one boat to ruin the peace and quiet for all around. Shock cord, gilguys of light line, or even halyard ends can be used to hold the halyards away from the mast by tying them off to the shrouds. It always amazes me that someone can sleep on a boat that has this noise going on. I've seen irate sailors march over to another boat in a marina and demand that the halyards be tied off, or, if no one is there, step aboard and do the job themselves.

Akin to the slapping halyard is what I call "Whistling Willie," the noise generated by a boat with a roller-furling mainsail. At anchor, these boats are OK, since they're headed into the wind, but in a marina slip, when the wind is at an angle across the mast, the noise is like that of a giant bottle top with the wind blowing across it, and the effect has a North Pole eeriness to it that seems very out of place in the Tropics. Boats with this rig can be equipped with a strip of cloth that can be run up the slot to kill the wind effect. This may be a nuisance to rig, but it should be well worth the trouble, both for those aboard and those on surrounding boats.

Boats like this are almost as annoying as the ones that are just to windward of you in a marina berth or at anchor and choose to run their engines right at cocktail hour. Diesel exhaust and hors d'oeuvres make an unhappy mix.

Hibachis

The use of hibachis, so prevalent in bareboat fleets, involves a few do's and don't's. A hibachi should never be used in a marina, at least on the boat. This is a dangerous practice and no marinas permit it. If one must be used, it should be taken ashore to a clear area away from all boats. In crowded harbors, it's dangerous to a boat close astern to have hibachi sparks blowing across it. Also, be careful in harbors with backwinding, where a sudden shift of breeze may send the sparks into your own cockpit.

Garbage

In the culinary department, garbage is a perpetual problem. Fortunately, most, but not all, yachtsmen are acutely aware of what the dumping of cans, plastic, and the like overboard can do to the charms of a harbor, especially considering the clarity of Caribbean water, and they are very careful to hold garbage until it can be disposed of ashore in a designated place. A supply of big, strong plastic garbage bags is important to have on board. They can be used to hold excess garbage in an out-of-the-way place on board until a disposal spot is reached.

Unfortunately, many European sailors and the local islanders are not so careful. At a lovely spot like Ile Pinel on the east coast of St. Martin, a beautiful little anchorage next to a picture-book island, the land on the island behind the golden strip of beach is a veritable garbage dump of old cans and trash left by local people who picnic there on weekends. In St. Barts, I gave a beer to a mechanic who had just finished working on our engine. He finished it and, before I could put it in our garbage, tossed the bottle blithely into the harbor. In Dominica, our crew took a big bag of garbage ashore at Portsmouth and asked some kids on the beach where to put it. They took it from him and just threw it under some palm trees back of the beach, where pigs soon lumbered over and started going at it.

Sunburn

I've mentioned sunburn, but it can't be stressed too much that care must be taken, especially in the first few days, not to overdo exposure. The proper sun lotion and very small doses of direct exposure should be combined, and the result will be a slowly acquired, comfortable tan that will look better. Even glare off the water can cause a burn. People with sensitive skin should wear a T-shirt while swimming, because the sun's rays penetrate water, too. Even though we spend about five months in the Caribbean each season, I put protective lotion on every day at 1000.

Hazards

Bugs are a sometime problem. Cockroaches are a fact of life, flies are present in many areas, and mosquitos come out in the fall rainy season and after a heavy spell of rain. A good repellent for application to the skin should be available, and sprays help keep the cabin clear. But beware of some European sprays that aren't on the approved U.S. list, as they're too strong for humans to inhale without damage to nasal passages. Baygone is one, and should be very carefully used, and not inhaled.

Underwater hazards are few. I've never seen a shark in the Caribbean, though there are some, of course, and

Practical Matters

I've heard of only a couple of isolated attacks in twenty-five years of sailing there. Barracuda look menacing, but seem to keep their own counsel. It's advisable, though, not to wear any shiny object like a bracelet or glittery ring while swimming or diving, as it might seem like the flash of a small fish to a barracuda. Sea urchins, the black, spiny orbs, have a painful, semipoisonous sting when stepped on, and should be carefully avoided. A blight reduced their population in the mid-Eighties, but they'll probably be back.

Man overboard is always a frightening consideration in sailing, and it's important to become familiar with the man-overboard equipment on board and the way it works. All this should be explained, especially when inexperienced guests are on a bareboat charter, and it's a good idea to stage a drill by tossing a box or cushion overboard and retrieving it. (The skipper should stand aside and let the crew handle it, just in case he's the one who happens to go overboard.) Not many life rings are equipped with a drogue—a small, conical, cloth sea anchor to keep the ring from blowing so fast with the surface wind that a swimmer can't keep up with it. It might be a good idea to have one rigged.

There has been considerable publicity about piracy and hijacking in the Caribbean, much of it connected with the drug trade. While incidents have occurred, the uninvolved visitor, charterer, or private boat owner should not be affected at all. But because of the publicity, the question of carrying firearms aboard has been raised. This is a matter of personal preference, but it does involve extra red tape during customs clearances. The U.S. Coast Guard may stop vessels and board them in some of the gateway passages, such as Anegada Passage, as part of the campaign to combat drug running.

Dinghies

Dinghies are a perpetual concern while cruising. The larger crewed charter yachts have solid launches on davits, and the bareboat fleets are universally equipped with husky, able, easily towed outboard dinghies. On private boats it's important to arrive at some solution that's compatible with the size of the boat and the conditions in which the dinghy will normally be operated.

For the bareboat fleets, towed dinghies are a fine solution, as bareboats are seldom out in water so rough that the dinghy is endangered. It's a great convenience to have the dinghy in the water and ready for use when arriving in port. But most towed dinghies are so big and sturdy that it would be impossible to get them aboard, so they're not a solution for those who want to keep the dinghy on deck for passaging.

Inflatables, which do not tow well for the most part, are one of the best answers. These are now available in towable form from some manufacturers. The boat must be fairly rigid, usually from bracing by floorboards, and have a modified V-shaped underbody to be towable. They adapt well to outboards, but very few make good rowboats. They're usually easier to stow on deck than rigid dinghies of the same size, or they can be deflated for long passages if they're not to do double duty as life rafts.

I've learned to lash down our eight-foot Avon, because once or twice when it was only secured topside by a painter, a sudden squall sent it kiting partway up the mast. The Avon can carry five people in calm water, but it's a tough job to row it into a strong breeze with any passengers aboard. It seems almost indestructible, but it's important to wash sand out of it and keep sand out of the valves. The valve caps are sometimes stolen, and

I've seen people using upended Heineken bottles as emergency valve caps.

When towing a rigid dinghy (or a shaped inflatable) the best distance astern seems to be just ahead of where the third wave of wake forms, but this rule of thumb can vary. Too long a painter will send a dinghy veering off into the wake, and a short one increases tension and strain. An eye should be kept peeled for water getting into the dinghy in rough conditions or heavy rain, as this can make it unmanageable. The outboard motor should be very securely clamped, with a safety line added if possible, and should be tipped up for towing. The gas tank should also be secured in place and the oars safely lashed or tucked under a seat. Always make sure that the dinghy painter is properly cleated on the yacht. A lost dinghy is a very expensive addition to bareboat charter costs, aside from the embarrassment and inconvenience. As a skipper, I've trained myself to check other people's knots and cleatings just in case. When I haven't, we've lost fenders, and once a dinghy was returned by a helpful soul anchored astern of us when he found it on its way from Philipsburg to Mexico.

Sails

The selection of sail combinations and the handling of them is vitally important to pleasant cruising. In Chapter III, I mentioned that my top recommendation for a manageable, flexible cruising rig is a cutter (double headrig) under forty feet, and a cutter or double headrig ketch over forty feet. In both these rigs, the sail combination can be adjusted in small or big increments, as the situation demands, for anything from light airs to a real blow. In contrast, cruising boats with a single big headsail are at a disadvantage when it comes time to reduce sail, even if it's a roller-furling sail. If the jibs are hanked on the forestay, a smaller jib can be substituted if it's part of the inventory, but this means foredeck work in sloppy conditions. If the big jib is a roller-furler and there's no other stay, the only solution is to furl it partially, but this doesn't work too well. Off the wind it's passable, but no matter how well it's cut, the shape won't be proper for going to windward, and, as pointed out, the center of effort has gone the wrong way—higher and forward. A private boat should certainly be equipped with an inventory of different-sized headsails, but on a bareboat with only one big sail, there are a couple of make-do solutions if caught in too much wind for full sail.

First, the main should be reefed. If this isn't enough, it's probably best to douse the main and go on jib alone before trying to reduce the jib size by partial furling. I've seen boats with this rig flogging along sadly by luffing the jib, and sometimes both sails, but this is no way to sail. If the jib finally becomes too much, the next step is probably to go back to reefed main alone. There won't be much windward progress this way, but the question then becomes one that involves the handling characteristics of the boat.

Different designs handle differently, of course, and these ideas are general ones for trying if you're not already familiar with a boat's handling properties. It might be a good idea to ask for guidance on this matter at the briefing sessions given by the charter operators. They're familiar with their own boats and should have the proper doctrine.

Reefing

On our cutter-rigged CSY, if we're trying to get the most out of her and get somewhere on schedule, the first step in reducing sail from the all-three combination of main, club-footed staysail, and roller-furling high-cut jib is to reef the main. I can do this by myself in about a minute with jiffy reefing, the system used on most charter boats. The sail is slacked off and supported by the topping lift, the halyard is slacked until a grommet on the luff at the reef line can be placed over a hook permanently installed at the gooseneck, and the clew reefing line, rigged through a block at the outer end of the boom, is taken in on a winch at the forward end of the boom. If you want to be able to double reef quickly, two clew reefing lines must be rigged. If you're organized, this really does take about a minute.

The sail is then reefed and ready to be trimmed. Be sure that the clew line is tightly snugged down on the boom, to keep the foot of the sail even and prevent a rip from the leech grommet serving as the new clew. The foot of the sail will then be in a loose flap along the boom, and to reduce windage and make things neater, reef points on the sail can be tied to bring this unused part into a snug furl.

In an increasing wind, reefing the main will have little effect on the boat's speed, but it will help stability and ease the feeling of tension and strain that comes with lugging too much sail and being overpowered. The next step can be to douse the staysail, or, if things are really piping up, the big jib can be furled and the staysail left flying. In this case, it might be a good idea to shake out the reef in the main for a bit more power. It can be reefed again if the breeze continues to increase. As can be seen, there are a good number of combinations possible through these three simple sails, and the only time anyone has to go forward of the mast is to douse the staysail. Often, we douse the jib and jog along under main and staysail to ease heeling at mealtime.

A helpful sail in a cruising inventory, though not provided on bareboat charters, is the one variously dubbed Flasher, Gennaker, Multiple Purpose Sail, Cruising Spinnaker, and other such names by various sailmakers. This is a poleless, lightweight sail, with all the color possibilities of a spinnaker. It's tacked down at the bow, and can be flown when the wind is just forward of the beam to broad on the quarter. Because there's no pole, it's not effective dead downwind, but it's a great sail to increase performance on the aforementioned points of sailing, which can sometimes be fairly dull under normal main and jib.

Another advantage of the double headrig is that on dead runs the club-footed staysail can be vanged out for wing-and-wing sailing. Admittedly, this isn't much added area, and far from a spinnaker, but it does add a mite of speed, looks better, and gives you the feeling that you're at least doing something to relieve the tedium of a dead run under main alone.

In a divided rig, the big advantage is to be able to get rid of the main quickly and completely and still have some driving power. "Jib and jigger" is a very comfortable off-the-wind combination in a strong breeze, and in light air the potential is there to play around with extra staysails.

Navigation

Navigation in the Caribbean isn't difficult. The eye is your most important piece of equipment, as you can see where you're going most of the time, and water color is very significant. Charter companies don't permit night operations (insurance runs out at sunset for bareboats under way) so it's not too important that there are few lighthouses, or that those that exist are sometimes un-

Practical Matters

reliable. Buoyage is spotty, though on the increase.

The American, British, and French charts covering the Caribbean are all right for plotting interisland passages, measuring distances, and taking bearings, but they're not, as a rule, very up to date on harbor details. Commercial charts are available for some areas, and the charter companies have planning charts that, when used in conjunction with the guide books (listed in the Bibliography), are sufficient. Some of the government charts are fascinating works of art in their detailing of topography and island profiles (it's interesting as well to see the dates when they were first made).

Some of the guide books listed in the bibliography are updated annually, others periodically. It's wise to get the latest one available for the area you intend to cruise, as nothing remains settled for very long in the matter of facilities, personnel, politics, and regulations. Even in a book of general information such as this one, certain information will eventually be superceded. Such is the volatile nature of things in the Caribbean. But this is not to write off the less frequently published books, as they can offer much helpful information. It's just that it's important to get the latest information whenever possible.

While lighthouses mean less to the average charter visitor than to private owners making interisland passages at night, buoyage is of concern to everyone, and it can be confusing. Some of the islands are on the "red-right-returning" American system, but others use the European (and worldwide) system, which is the reverse. Be sure to find out ahead of time which system is in use before heading into a new area. This is information that must be found in regularly updated publications, because changes are being made frequently. The B.V.I. went to the American system in 1984, a year later than the announced date for doing it, and some guide books published in 1983 reported on the changes a year ahead of time. The new channel at Mamora Bay, Antigua, buoyed in late 1984, uses the American system, too.

Eyeballing

By far the most important navigational guide in most areas is the color of the water. If it's deep blue, there's no trouble. A somewhat brighter, paler blue is all right, too. When it starts to be pale green, or even white, the margin is down very close. When entering a fairly shallow harbor, it's sometimes hard to tell whether dark patches are cloud shadows, grass, or reefs; this can only come from experience. As explained in Chapter VIII, always look for clear sand, which makes the water above it much paler than that over grass, when choosing a spot to drop the anchor.

Reefs can usually be seen well when the sun is high and light is good. Try to avoid areas where eyeballing through reefs is necessary when the sun is in your eyes or the sky is dark; it's much harder then to see the telltale underwater colors. A reef or coral head that's black is usually deep enough not to menace a yacht of average draft. When it begins to appear brown, look out, and when it's a yellowish brown, stay away. In open water where there's a swell, most reefs shallow enough to bother a yacht will break periodically, but this doesn't happen, of course, in calm harbors. The judicious use of depth sounders is always a great help.

Visual Piloting

Visibility is usually very good in the Caribbean, except in rain squalls or periods of African dust (which seem to be occurring more frequently due to the severe drought conditions there). These conditions can cut down visibility to less than five miles, but it's usually from ten miles to unlimited, and interisland passages merely mean setting a compass course and making sure that the next island shows up where it should be.

Laying a direct compass course won't always get the desired result, as currents must be considered, and they're unpredictable. Anegada Passage is famous for its dilatory currents. I've experienced both northerly and southerly sets in it for no rhyme or reason. In addition to fouling up dead reckoning, currents there also cause the most wicked, confused sea conditions in the Caribbean.

There's often a westerly set of currents, generated by the constant trade winds, in the passages between the major islands of the Lesser Antilles. Once an island is sighted ahead, it's a good idea to see if it keeps the same bearing while you hold your course. If you have to harden up to the eastward to hold the same point on the target island, you're being set. The last time I came from Guadeloupe to Antigua, with African dust cutting visibility sharply, I allowed five degrees for westerly set and ended up five degrees high of the Antigua landfall, so one never knows.

Except for the fun of doing it, celestial navigation isn't really needed in island cruising in the Caribbean, though it would of course be needed on a direct run from Panama across to the Virgins, or on any open-water passage out of sight of land for a couple of days. Loran has not been programmed to the Caribbean as of this writing. RDF can be used to check bearings on commercial stations, as each island has one, and Radio Antilles on Montserrat can be heard all over the Caribbean.

Communications

The radio is useful for news and weather, and it's possible to keep up with world news and general U.S. news, if not the police blotter from your hometown, from many stations throughout the Caribbean. The U.S. Virgin Islands and Puerto Rico have typical American stations with news from the major broadcasting systems, Radio Antilles covers the entire Caribbean, and each island has its own radio station (as well as a TV station on most). You can practice your Spanish and French, if you want to, by listening to stations broadcasting in those languages. We've watched the Super Bowl in the B.V.I., and you can almost always hear a cricket broadcast on the local British or ex-British islands.

New York and Miami newspapers are delivered, at a price, to the areas that have direct jet service (the weekday *New York Times* is $2.75 in Tortola), and the *Paris Herald* is available in Guadeloupe and Martinique. Latin American editions of the news magazines are generally available in larger towns and airports.

As for individual communications from yachts, VHF radio is the lifeline of the Caribbean. The bareboat charter fleets live by it; each company designates a certain channel for keeping in touch with their own boats. It's like listening to back-fence gossip to have on one of these channels and hear chatter about overheating engines, airplane reconfirmations, inquiries about lost luggage, and dinner reservations. Channel 16 is the contact and emergency channel, and should not be used for any other purposes. Once contact is made, a channel to be switched to is agreed upon. Channels 68 and 06 are used most often, but many others are available.

Practical Matters

Correct radio procedures should be followed, and most people are pretty good at it, if a bit informal. But you do hear some howlers. (We had one once when our daughter called us from another boat, following all the correct procedures. My wife picked up our microphone, and with no procedure patter at all, merely said, "Hello, Alice, this is Mother.")

VHF is used constantly for ship-to-shore contact and subsequent telephone connections to such stations as Virgin Island Radio, Radio Tortola, and Radio Saba, plus others down the line.

Vessels equipped with single-sideband radio, which most bareboats don't have but most crewed boats do, can make direct connections with operators in the States or major Caribbean islands. Ham radio operators are a separate breed and have their own worldwide network. Ham is becoming increasingly popular on private boats.

Unless you're off in an isolated area for a considerable time, it's possible to make direct phone calls to the rest of the world from land telephones (most of the islands are in the 809 area code). It's relatively simple to get through to the States with credit-card or collect calls. In the French islands, however, pay cash if possible, because collect calls take several hours and credit cards are no go. Sometimes the connections are not the best, but in general the service throughout the Caribbean is surprisingly good. Indeed, it's often easier to call the States than to make a local call.

Mail can be a problem to anyone spending some time in the Caribbean, although this shouldn't be a worry for charter customers. Even on a two-week charter, visitors are most likely down and back before a letter can reach them, and they always beat home the postcards they mail. (Stamp collecting, incidentally, is popular among many visitors, and some islands, like the B.V.I. and Grenada, cater to this hobby with frequent issues of exotically illustrated stamps.)

For sailors cruising for longer periods, most of the marinas in the popular centers like St. Thomas, Tortola, Antigua, and St. Lucia will act as mail drops and hold mail addressed to people on boats. As mentioned earlier, mail is slow in both directions, so some of the busier centers have courier services, the best way to send important mail quickly.

Finances

The various Caribbean currencies were covered in Chapter VI. Visitors on a charter of a week or two should bring a bit more money than they think necessary, mostly in traveler's checks, and, as stated, U.S. money is universally accepted. If you miscalculate and do run short, either on a short visit or a long one, it's possible to refinance in several ways. Banks in many of the islands will sell traveler's checks against a credit card, and American Express offices will also arrange for checks or cash for card holders. Some of the bigger American banks have offices throughout the Caribbean, and people with accounts at the home offices may be able to cash a check or obtain traveler's checks here. Some marinas will cash checks for properly identified yachtsmen.

Medical

If you have a special medication, it's important to bring a supply for your entire stay, as it's time-consuming and not always practical to get prescriptions filled. But every island of any size has a hospital with an emergency room, so minor injuries and illnesses can usually be handled locally. Some of the bigger hotels have doctors on call, and help can be arranged through a hotel, or even through a cruise ship, if there's a serious emergency. San Juan has big-city facilities, and problems that can't be handled at the smaller island hospitals can be taken care of there. (San Juan has air connections with almost every island, and, in a serious emergency, air charters are available throughout the Caribbean.)

Some of the smaller settlements, like Gun Creek on Gorda Sound (one we've used) have clinics that are equipped to handle routine problems quite competently. Drugstores are found in all but the smallest islands and are usually fairly well stocked. In the French islands, brand names and drug names are often quite different from American ones.

Dental problems are not always easily solved, as dentists aren't widely available and standards may not be high. Yachts should be equipped with emergency dental kits, but a serious crisis would probably mean travel to one of the bigger cities or an early return home.

As an obvious word of caution, controlled substances are illegal in all islands, and Caribbean jails are not noted for their amenities. As for running inadvertently into drug drops or drug traffic, documented instances of yachtsmen experiencing this are almost nil.

X

Suggested Itineraries

Infinite variations are possible on cruising itineraries in the Caribbean, and a lifetime of cruising would hardly exhaust them. A cruise can be a relaxing jog between anchorages that are three miles apart, with stops for lunch and swimming in between overnight ports in an area like the B.V.I., or it can be a series of long open-water reaches between the big islands of the Lesser Antilles. Much depends on the makeup of the crew and the kind of sailing being sought. There are more relaxers than hairy-chested passage-makers, especially among the charter fleets, and in the areas where one long day's sail is a necessity, it might be smart instead to stay in port and sight-see, snorkel, or just sunbathe and read about the next one.

Some crews may want to go from casino to nightclub (not too easy to find in most areas) to casino, with marina stops as often as possible, while others may seek the solitude of a lonely cove or isolated reef. Food fanciers may want a different restaurant every night. Serious diving enthusiasts have their own special requirements, and they're wise to use boats that cater to diving operations.

The most important rule about any cruising itinerary is not to try to do too much. If there's doubt, err on the side of fewer hours spent under way and less distance to be covered, as nothing can spoil a potentially pleasant cruise more quickly than a series of overtiring days

Suggested Itineraries

spent in pushing to distant objectives. We've made some really long day's runs in ranging the islands, but followed them with rest days or short runs. A seventy-two-mile, twelve-and-a-half-hour passage from Antigua to St. Barts took the distance prize for us. Another long push is Fort de France to Portsmouth, Dominica, sixty-five miles with little chance of stopping elsewhere except the less-than-comfortable mooring spot south of Roseau. But at least there's sightseeing along Dominica's startling array of peaks. The run to St. Barts has only the distant purple smudges of Nevis, St. Kitts, and Statia to vary the horizon (though the fact that it's mostly glorious, fast reaching is a big help). If someone complains about the motion in this kind of exhilarating, open-water sailing, tell them they're getting instant, automatic isometric exercise without even having to think about it, because just in adapting to the motion, many muscles are brought into play.

Focusing on the main charter centers of St. Thomas, Tortola, St. Martin, Antigua, St. Lucia, and Grenada, I've listed some sample itineraries that take in the best and most popular ports (plus two for the western Caribbean), but merely as a guide to planning. All sorts of variations can be worked on these, according to personal choice, and they may be combined with longer cruises in some cases. I haven't included the Grand-Terre half of Guadeloupe or the east coast of Martinique, since I haven't been to either area, and few boats ever do seem to get there. Besides, Julius Wilensky, the tirelessly energetic author of cruising guides (see Bibliography), covers circumnavigating Martinique in his guide to that area, and ends up saying "Now that I've done it, I see no reason for circumnavigating Martinique."

In only a few cases, where there's no other choice,

have I listed runs of more than forty miles; and those of thirty and under are used as much as possible. On the long runs, with the boat zipping along in the trades and a new island looming purple ahead, you can pretend you're Columbus, discovering new islands on each day's run.

These itineraries are suggestions for taking in most of the Caribbean's best cruising harbors. In each one of them, there is at least one day with little or no distance to cover to take advantage of spots like Tobago Cays, The Baths, Anguilla, Half Moon Reef, Norman Island caves, and many more that are worth at least a day of leisurely exploring and enjoyment. Fast, exhilarating sails in the trades are part of these itineraries, too. Days that combine exploring and sailing are the essence of the Caribbean's great cruising.

The following table of distances should be a help in figuring out the cruising distances on the itineraries.

Port-to-Port Distances (in nautical miles)

Heading east and then south

San Juan–Fajardo	33
Fajardo–Culebra	18
Culebra–Charlotte Amalie	20
Charlotte Amalie–Road Town	20
Road Town–Gorda Sound	18
Gorda Sound–St. Martin	80
St. Martin–Anguilla (Road Bay)	13
St. Martin–St. Barts	16
St. Barts–St. John, Antigua	72
St. Barts–Nevis	55
Nevis–English Harbour	50
St. John–English Harbour	16

Suggested Itineraries

English Harbour–DesHayes	42
DesHayes–Iles des Saintes	31
Iles des Saintes–Portsmouth	20
Portsmouth–Roseau	19
Roseau–Fort de France	46
Fort de France–Anse d'Arlet	7
Anse d'Arlet–Castries	36
Castries–Marigot	4
Marigot–Cumberland Bay	44
Cumberland Bay–Blue Lagoon	11
Blue Lagoon–Bequia	8
Bequia–Cannouan	20
Cannouan–Tobago Cays	6
Tobago Cays–Union	4
Union–Tyrell Bay	10
Tyrell Bay–St. George's	30

St. Thomas: One week in American waters

First day, 38 miles west to Fajardo
Second day, 18 miles east to Culebra (windward work)
Third day, exploring Ensenada Honda
Fourth day, 25 miles to Christmas Cove (windward work)
Fifth day, 5 miles to Trunk Bay for swim and snorkeling at lunch, 2 miles to Francis Bay for overnight
Sixth day, 10 miles to Hurricane Hole for exploring and choice of anchorage
Seventh day, 15 miles back to Charlotte Amalie along south coast of St. John
(Alternative: To avoid windward work, go only as far as Culebra and stop at Great Cruz Bay or Caneel Bay on way back to Charlotte Amalie.)

St. Thomas: One week into British Virgin Islands

First day, 8 miles Charlotte Amalie to Christmas Cove
Second day, 10 miles to Jost Van Dyke to enter B.V.I., swim

at Sandy Cay, overnight Great Harbor or Little Harbor
Third day, 12 miles to Marina Cay or Trellis Bay
Fourth day, 10 miles to Gorda Sound
Fifth day, 8 miles to Baths for lunch and 10 miles to Peter Island for night
Sixth day, 3 miles to Norman Island caves for lunch and overnight at The Bight, Norman Island
Seventh day, 18 miles back to Charlotte Amalie

(This can be made a two-week cruise, combining St. John harbors coming and going, or spending more time in B.V.I. visiting Virgin Gorda Yacht Harbour, Road Town, Cooper Island, and Cane Garden Bay.)

Road Town, Tortola, British Virgin Islands: One week in British Virgin Islands

First day, 9 miles to Trellis Bay
Second day. 10 miles to Gorda Sound
Third day, 8 miles to Baths for lunch, 2 miles to Virgin Gorda Yacht Harbour for night
Fourth day, 13 miles to Norman Island, the night after stop at the caves
Fifth day, 10 miles to Sandy Cay for lunch swim, 2 miles to Great Harbor, Jost Van Dyke, or Cane Garden Bay for night (avoid Cane Garden in northerly swells)
Sixth day, 12 miles to Peter Island for night
Seventh day, lunch at Deadman's Bay, then 3 miles back to base

(If starting from Nanny Cay, it is 2 miles west of Road Town, and if from Maya Cove, it is 3 miles east. Alternate harbors in the B.V.I. include Marina Cay, Drake's Anchorage, Leverick Bay, Cooper Island, White Bay, Great Harbour, Peter Island, Benures Bay, and such lunch stops as The Dogs, Green Cay, Salt Island village, and the wreck of the steamship *Rhone* off its west end for diving.)

Suggested Itineraries

Road Town, Tortola: Two weeks in British Virgin Islands and American Virgin Islands

Combine the above with a circumnavigation of St. John, clearing B.V.I. at Road Town or West End and entering U.S. at Cruz Bay.

(Some people like Gorda Sound so much they spend several days at its several anchorages, exploring surrounding reefs and islands by dinghy.)

Philipsburg, St. Martin: One week in surrounding islands

First day, 12 miles to Marigot, French St. Martin
Second day, 10 miles to Road Bay, Anguilla
Third day, at Anguilla (Crocus Bay or Sandy Island or Prickly Pears)
Fourth day, 13 miles to Grand Case, St. Martin
Fifth day, 6 miles to Ile Pinel
Sixth day, 13 miles to St. Barts
Seventh day, 16 miles return

(With more time, stops can be made at Simson Bay, Dutch St. Martin, Marcel Bay, French St. Martin, Ile Fourche, and in exploring ashore at Marigot and Gustavia, St. Bart.)

Antigua: One-island cruise

Depending on time available, choice of Falmouth, Carlisle Bay (or Curtain Bluff), Five Islands, Deep Bay, Dickinson Bay, St. John's (for shopping), Barbuda, Parham Sound, Green Island, and Mamora Bay. A week or more can easily be spent on this circuit of the island.

(From Antigua north to Nevis, St. Kitts, Statia, St. Barts, St. Martin, and Barbuda is only for those who enjoy long passages between surgy harbors and windward work in returning, no matter in which direction the circuit is made.)

Antigua north: One-way trip (or reverse)

First day, 50 miles to Nevis
Second day, 11 miles to St. Kitts
Third day, 48 miles to St. Barts

Antigua: One week south to St. Lucia (reverse north from there)

First day, 42 miles to DesHayes, Guadeloupe
Second day, 31 miles to Iles des Saintes
Third day, 20 miles to Portsmouth, Dominica
Fourth day, 19 miles to Roseau or Woodbridge Bay
Fifth day, 46 miles to Fort de France
Sixth day, 7 miles to Anse d'Arlet
Seventh day, 40 miles to Marigot Bay

St. Lucia: One week south to Grenada (or second week from Antigua)

First day, 10 miles Marigot to Soufrière or Pitons
Second day, 44 miles to Cumberland or Wallilabou Bays
Third day, 15 miles to Admiralty Bay, Bequia
Fourth day, 26 miles to Tobago Cays
Fifth day, layover at Tobago Cays and 4 miles to Union
Sixth day, 7 miles to Hillsborough and 4 miles to Tyrell Bay
Seventh day, 30 miles to St. George's

St. Lucia: One week and return to base

First day, 8 miles to Pigeon Island
Second day, 33 miles to Fort de France
Third day, in Fort de France and 3 miles to Anse Mitan
Fourth day, 7 miles to Anse d'Arlet
Fifth day, 26 miles to Rodney Bay

Suggested Itineraries

Sixth day, 18 miles to Pitons
Seventh day, 10 miles to Marigot
(To the Grenadines and back in one week from St. Lucia involves long passages, but can be done. Two weeks is much better for that.)

St. Vincent: One week and return to base from Blue Lagoon

First day, 8 miles to Admiralty Bay
Second day, 20 miles to Cannouan
Third day, 6 miles to Tobago Cays to spend day
Fourth day, 4 miles to Mayreau, Clifton, or Petit St. Vincent
Fifth day, between Mayreau, Clifton, PSV, or Palm Island
Sixth day, 25 miles to Mustique
Seventh day, 15 miles return to Blue Lagoon

St. Vincent: One week south to Grenada (or reverse from there)

First five days, same as above
Sixth day, 9 miles to Tyrell Bay via Hillsborough
Seventh day, 30 miles to St. George's

Grenada: One week and return to base at the Lagoon, St. George's

First day, exploring south coast, choice of anchorages
Second day, 10 miles to Halifax
Third day, 27 miles to Tyrell Bay
Fourth day, 9 miles to Clifton, then Mayreau or PSV
Fifth day, 4 miles to Tobago Cays and spend day
Sixth day, 14 miles to Tyrell Bay with stop at Sandy Cay
Seventh day, 30 miles to St. George's
(If start is from L'Anse aux Epines, it is 7 miles from St. George's around Grenada's southern end on south coast.)

Bay Islands of Honduras: One week out of Brick Harbor, Roatan, and return

First three days, eastward along south coast, exploring French Harbor, Caribe Point Bight, Oak Ridge, and Port Royal (good diving), all about 5 miles apart
Fourth day, 20 miles to Cochinos Cays
Fifth day, 18 miles to Utila Cays
Sixth day, 18 miles to Anthony's Cay
Seventh day, return to base

Belize: One-week cruise on the barrier reef

First four days, 30 miles to Lighthouse Reef to Blue Hole and Half Moon Cay (great diving)
Fifth day, 20 miles to Sitee River
Sixth day, 12 miles to Tobacco Cay
Seventh day, return to base

Bibliography

Fenger, Frederic A. *Alone in the Caribbean.* Belmont, Mass.: Wellington Books, 1912; reissued 1958.
———. *The Cruise of the Diablesse.* Belmont, Mass.: Wellington Books, 1926; reissued 1958.
Hart, Jerrems C., and William T. Stone. *A Cruising Guide to the Caribbean and the Bahamas.* New York: Dodd, Mead & Company, 1982.
Mitchell, Carleton. *Islands to Windward: Cruising the Caribbean.* New York: D. Van Nostrand Co., 1948, 1955.
Morison, Samuel Eliot. *The European Discovery of America: The Southern Voyages,* 1492–1616. New York: Oxford University Press, 1974.
Robinson, Bill. *Islands.* New York: Dodd, Mead & Company, 1985.
———. *South to the Caribbean.* New York: W. W. Norton & Company, 1982.
———. *Where to Cruise.* New York: W. W. Norton & Company, 1984.
Seyfarth, Fritz. *Tales of the Caribbean.* New York: John de Graff, Inc.
Street, Donald M., Jr. *Street's Cruising Guides to the Eastern Caribbean.* Volumes I, III. New York: W. W. Norton & Co.
———. *Street's Cruising Guides to the Eastern Caribbean.* Volume II, Parts 1 and 2. New York: W. W. Norton & Co., 1985.
Wouk, Herman. *Don't Stop the Carnival.* New York: Doubleday & Co.

List of Cruising Guides

Antigua-Barbuda Marine Guide
c/o Antigua Yacht Club
English Harbour
Antigua, West Indies

Free. Updated annually.

Cruising Guide to the Virgin Islands
by Simon and Nancy Scott

1305 U.S. 19S
Suite 402
Clearwater, FL 33456

Price: $9.95. Updated periodically; last update was in 1985.

St. Maarten/St. Martin Area Cruising Guide
Edited by William J. Eiman

239 Delancey Street
Philadelphia, PA 19106

Price: $10.00. Includes Anguilla, St. Barts, and Saba. Updated periodically.

Sailor's Guide to the Windward Islands
by Chris Doyle

Box 17
St. Vincent, West Indies

Price: $6.50. Also available through bareboat companies. Updated periodically; last update was in 1984.

List of Cruising Guides

Yachtsman's Guide to the Bay Islands of Honduras
by Julius M. Wilensky

Caribbean Sailing Yachts
Box 491
Tenafly, NJ 07670

Price: $17.25. Updated periodically.

Yachtsman's Guide to the Greater Antilles
Edited by Harry Kline

Box 61141
North Miami, FL 33161

Price: $9.95. The 1982 edition is the most current for the Dominican Republic and Haiti.

Yachtsman's Guide to Puerto Rico and the Virgin Islands
Edited by Harry Kline

Box 61141
North Miami, FL 33161

Price: $12.50. Updated annually.

Yachtsman's Guide to the Windward Islands
by Julius M. Wilensky

Caribbean Sailing Yachts
Box 491
Tenafly, NJ 07670

Price: $19.95. Updated periodically.